THE
CANTERBURY PUZZLES

AND OTHER CURIOUS PROBLEMS

BY

HENRY ERNEST DUDENEY

FOURTH EDITION

(With Some Fuller Solutions and Additional Notes)

DOVER PUBLICATIONS, INC.
NEW YORK • NEW YORK

This Dover edition, first published in 1958, is an unabridged republication of the fourth edition as originally published by Thomas Nelson & Sons, Limited. A new note on British coins and stamps has been added to this Dover edition, which is published through special arrangement with Thomas Nelson & Sons, Limited.

International Standard Book Number: 0-486-20474-X
Library of Congress Catalog Card Number: 58-13361

Manufactured in the United States of America
Dover Publications, Inc.
180 Varick Street
New York, N. Y. 10014

CONTENTS

v

This edition is dedicated to the memory of

Henry E. Dudeney

1847 – 1930

with the hope that it will keep alive for many years his remarkable contributions to intellectual and mathematical recreations.

PREFACE

WHEN preparing this new edition for the press, my first inclination was to withdraw a few puzzles that appeared to be of inferior interest, and to substitute others for them. But, on second thoughts, I decided to let the book stand in its original form and add extended solutions and some short notes to certain problems that have in the past involved me in correspondence with interested readers who desired additional information.

I have also provided—what was clearly needed for reference—an index. The very nature and form of the book prevented any separation of the puzzles into classes, but a certain amount of classification will be found in the index. Thus, for example, if the reader has a predilection for problems with Moving Counters, or for Magic Squares, or for Combination and Group Puzzles, he will find that in the index these are brought together for his convenience.

Though the problems are quite different, with the exception of just one or two little variations or extensions, from those in my book *Amusements in Mathematics*, each work being complete in itself, I have thought it would help the reader who happens to have both books before him if I made occasional references that would direct him to solutions and analyses in the later book calculated to elucidate matter in these pages. ·This course has also obviated the necessity of my repeating myself. For the sake of brevity, *Amusements in Mathematics* is throughout referred to as *A. in M.*

HENRY E. DUDENEY.

THE AUTHORS' CLUB,
July 2, 1919.

7

A Note on British Coins and Stamps

SEVERAL of Dudeney's puzzles are based upon British money, which might not be familiar to the American reader. The basic unit is the pound, which contains twenty shillings; the shilling in turn contains twelve pence (pennies). The symbol for pound is £, which is placed before the number like our dollar sign. The symbols for shilling and pence are, respectively, s. and d., which are placed, like our cent sign, after the number. In place notation these symbols are sometimes omitted. Common ways of writing British prices are:

£2–6–6	Two pounds, six shillings, six pence
2 6 6	Two pounds, six shillings, six pence
7/6 or 7–6	or 7 s. 6 d., seven shillings and six pence.

Just as in American money one does not write down 101¢, but $1.01, in British notation one writes down twenty-five shillings as £1 5 s.; eighteen pence as 1 s. 6 d.; and twelve pence as 1 s.

At the time that Dudeney wrote his books British coinage was not exactly the same as it is today. These coins could have been available to his readers:

Name	Notation	Value
Farthing	¼ d.	One quarter of a penny
Half penny	½ d.	One half of a penny
Penny	1 d.	
Two pence	2 d.	Two pence (1/6th of a shilling)
Three pence	3 d.	Three pence (1/4th of a shilling)
Four pence	4 d.	Four pence (1/3rd of a shilling)
Six pence	6 d.	Six pence (1/2 of a shilling)

9

Name	Notation	Value
Shilling	1 s.	Twelve pence
Florin	2 s.	Two shillings
Half crown	2 s. 6 d.	Two shillings and six pence
Double florin	4 s.	Four shillings
Crown	5 s.	Five shillings
Half sovereign	10 s.	Ten shillings (half a pound)
Sovereign	£1	Twenty shillings or one pound
Guinea	£1 1 s.	Twenty-one shillings

Many of these coins are no longer in circulation. The guinea, even though the coin itself is no longer in circulation, is still used as a value term for £1 1 s., and its exact multiples. £5 5 s., for example, is still spoken of as five guineas.

The postal stamps in circulation in Dudeney's time were of the following denominations: ½ d., 1 d., 1½ d., 2 d., 2½ d., 3 d., 4 d., 5 d., 6 d., 9 d., 10 d., 1 s., 2 s. 6 d., 5 s., 10 s., £1, £5.

INTRODUCTION

READERS of *The Mill on the Floss* will remember that whenever Mr. Tulliver found himself confronted by any little difficulty he was accustomed to make the trite remark, " It's a puzzling world." There can be no denying the fact that we are surrounded on every hand by posers, some of which the intellect of man has mastered, and many of which may be said to be impossible of solution. Solomon himself, who may be supposed to have been as sharp as most men at solving a puzzle, had to admit " there be three things which are too wonderful for me ; yea, four which I know not : the way of an eagle in the air ; the way of a serpent upon a rock ; the way of a ship in the midst of the sea ; and the way of a man with a maid."

Probing into the secrets of Nature is a passion with all men ; only we select different lines of research. Men have spent long lives in such attempts as to turn the baser metals into gold, to discover perpetual motion, to find a cure for certain malignant diseases, and to navigate the air.

From morning to night we are being perpetually brought face to face with puzzles. But there are puzzles and puzzles. Those that are usually devised for recreation and pastime may be roughly divided into two classes : Puzzles that are built up on some interesting or informing little principle ; and puzzles that conceal no principle whatever—such as a picture cut at random into little bits to be put together again, or the juvenile imbecility known as the " rebus," or " picture puzzle." The former species may be said to be adapted to the amusement of the sane man or woman ; the latter can be confidently recommended to the feeble-minded.

The curious propensity for propounding puzzles is not peculiar to any race or to any period of history. It is simply innate in every intelligent man, woman, and child that has ever lived, though it is always showing itself in different forms ; whether the individual be a Sphinx of Egypt, a Samson of Hebrew lore, an Indian fakir, a Chinese philosopher, a mahatma of Tibet, or a European mathematician makes little difference.

Theologian, scientist, and artisan are perpetually engaged in attempting to solve puzzles, while every game, sport, and pastime is built up of problems of greater or less difficulty. The spontaneous question asked by the child of his parent, by one cyclist of another while taking a brief rest on a stile, by a cricketer during the luncheon hour, or by a yachtsman lazily scanning the horizon, is frequently a problem of considerable difficulty. In short, we are all propounding puzzles to one another every day of our lives— without always knowing it.

A good puzzle should demand the exercise of our best wit and ingenuity, and although a knowledge of mathematics and a certain familiarity with the methods of logic are often of great service in the solution of these things, yet it sometimes happens that a kind of natural cunning and sagacity is of considerable value. For many of the best problems cannot be solved by any familiar scholastic methods, but must be attacked on entirely original lines. This is why, after a long and wide experience, one finds that particular puzzles will sometimes be solved more readily by persons possessing only naturally alert faculties than by the better educated. The best players of such puzzle games as chess and draughts are not mathematicians, though it is just possible that often they may have undeveloped mathematical minds.

It is extraordinary what fascination a good puzzle has for a great many people. We know the thing to be of trivial importance, yet we are impelled to master it ; and when we have succeeded there is a pleasure and a sense of satisfaction that are a quite sufficient reward for our trouble, even when there is no prize to be won. What is this mysterious charm that many find irresistible ?

Why do we like to be puzzled ? The curious thing is that directly the enigma is solved the interest generally vanishes. We have done it, and that is enough. But why did we ever attempt to do it ?

The answer is simply that it gave us pleasure to seek the solution —that the pleasure was all in the seeking and finding for their own sakes. A good puzzle, like virtue, is its own reward. Man loves to be confronted by a mystery, and he is not entirely happy until he has solved it. We never like to feel our mental inferiority to those around us. The spirit of rivalry is innate in man ; it stimulates the smallest child, in play or education, to keep level with his fellows, and in later life it turns men into great discoverers, inventors, orators, heroes, artists, and (if they have more material aims) perhaps millionaires.

In starting on a tour through the wide realm of Puzzledom we do well to remember that we shall meet with points of interest of a very varied character. I shall take advantage of this variety. People often make the mistake of confining themselves to one little corner of the realm, and thereby miss opportunities of new pleasures that lie within their reach around them. One person will keep to acrostics and other word puzzles, another to mathematical brain-rackers, another to chess problems (which are merely puzzles on the chess-board, and have little practical relation to the game of chess), and so on. This is a mistake, because it restricts one's pleasures, and neglects that variety which is so good for the brain.

And there is really a practical utility in puzzle-solving. Regular exercise is supposed to be as necessary for the brain as for the body, and in both cases it is not so much what we do as the doing of it from which we derive benefit. The daily walk recommended by the doctor for the good of the body, or the daily exercise for the brain, may in itself appear to be so much waste of time ; but it is the truest economy in the end. Albert Smith, in one of his amusing novels, describes a woman who was convinced that she suffered from " cobwigs on the brain." This may be a very rare complaint, but in a more metaphorical sense many of us are very apt to suffer from mental cobwebs, and there is nothing equal to the solving of puzzles and problems for sweeping them away. They keep the brain alert, stimulate the imagination, and develop the reasoning faculties. And not only are they useful in this indirect way, but they often directly help us by teaching us some little tricks and " wrinkles " that can be applied in the affairs of life at the most unexpected times and in the most unexpected ways.

There is an interesting passage in praise of puzzles in the quaint letters of Fitzosborne. Here is an extract : " The ingenious study of making and solving puzzles is a science undoubtedly of most necessary acquirement, and deserves to make a part in the meditation of both sexes. It is an art, indeed, that I would recommend to the encouragement of both the Universities, as it affords the easiest and shortest method of conveying some of the most useful principles of logic. It was the maxim of a very wise prince that ' he who knows not how to dissemble knows not how to reign ' ; and I desire you to receive it as mine, that ' he who knows not how to riddle knows not how to live.' "

How are good puzzles invented ? I am not referring to acrostics, anagrams, charades, and that sort of thing, but to puzzles that contain an original idea. Well, you cannot invent a good puzzle to order, any more than you can invent anything else in that manner. Notions for puzzles come at strange times and in strange ways. They are suggested by something we see or hear, and are led up to by other puzzles that come under our notice. It is useless to say, " I will sit down and invent an original puzzle," because there is no way of creating an idea ; you can only make use of it when it comes. You may think this is wrong, because an expert in these things will make scores of puzzles while another person, equally clever, cannot invent one " to save his life," as we say. The explanation is very simple. The expert knows an idea when he sees one, and is able by long experience to judge of its value. Fertility, like facility, comes by practice.

Sometimes a new and most interesting idea is suggested by the blunder of somebody over another puzzle. A boy was given a puzzle to solve by a friend, but he misunderstood what he had to do, and set about attempting what most likely everybody would have told him was impossible. But he was a boy with a will, and he stuck at it for six months, off and on, until he actually succeeded. When his friend saw the solution, he said, " This is not the puzzle I intended—you misunderstood me—but you have found out something much greater ! " And the puzzle which that boy accidentally discovered is now in all the old puzzle books.

Puzzles can be made out of almost anything, in the hands of the ingenious person with an idea. Coins, matches, cards, counters, bits of wire or string, all come in useful. An immense number of puzzles have been made out of the letters of the alphabet, and from those nine little digits and cipher, 1, 2, 3, 4, 5, 6, 7, 8, 9, and 0.

It should always be remembered that a very simple person may propound a problem that can only be solved by clever heads—if at all. A child asked, " Can God do everything ? " On receiving an affirmative reply, she at once said : " Then can He make a stone so heavy that He can't lift it ? " Many wide-awake grown-up people do not at once see a satisfactory answer. Yet the difficulty lies merely in the absurd, though cunning, form of the question, which really amounts to asking, " Can the Almighty destroy His own omnipotence ? " It is somewhat similar to the other question, " What would happen if an irresistible moving body came in contact with an immovable body ? " Here we have simply a contradiction in terms, for if there existed such a thing as an immovable body, there could not at the same time exist a moving body that nothing could resist.

Professor Tyndall used to invite children to ask him puzzling questions, and some of them were very hard nuts to crack. One child asked him why that part of a towel that was dipped in water was of a darker colour than the dry part. How many readers could give the correct reply? Many people are satisfied with the most ridiculous answers to puzzling questions. If you ask, " Why can we see through glass ? " nine people out of ten will reply,

" Because it is transparent ; " which is, of course, simply another way of saying, " Because we can see through it."

Puzzles have such an infinite variety that it is sometimes very difficult to divide them into distinct classes. They often so merge in character that the best we can do is to sort them into a few broad types. Let us take three or four examples in illustration of what I mean.

First there is the ancient Riddle, that draws upon the imagination and play of fancy. Readers will remember the riddle of the Sphinx, the monster of Bœotia who propounded enigmas to the inhabitants and devoured them if they failed to solve them. It was said that the Sphinx would destroy herself if one of her riddles was ever correctly answered. It was this : " What animal walks on four legs in the morning, two at noon, and three in the evening ? " It was explained by Œdipus, who pointed out that man walked on his hands and feet in the morning of life, at the noon of life he walked erect, and in the evening of his days he supported his infirmities with a stick. When the Sphinx heard this explanation, she dashed her head against a rock and immediately expired. This shows that puzzle solvers may be really useful on occasion.

Then there is the riddle propounded by Samson. It is perhaps the first prize competition in this line on record, the prize being thirty sheets and thirty changes of garments for a correct solution. The riddle was this : " Out of the eater came forth meat, and out of the strong came forth sweetness." The answer was, " A honeycomb in the body of a dead lion." To-day this sort of riddle survives in such a form as, " Why does a chicken cross the road ? " to which most people give the answer, " To get to the other side ; " though the correct reply is, " To worry the chauffeur." It has degenerated into the conundrum, which is usually based on a mere pun. For example, we have been asked from our infancy, " When is a door not a door ? " and here again the answer usually furnished (" When it is a-jar ") is not the correct one. It should be, " When it is a negress (an egress)."

There is the large class of Letter Puzzles, which are based on the little peculiarities of the language in which they are written—such as anagrams, acrostics, word-squares, and charades. In this class we also find palindromes, or words and sentences that read backwards and forwards alike. These must be very ancient indeed, if it be true that Adam introduced himself to Eve (in the English language, be it noted) with the palindromic words, " Madam, I'm Adam," to which his consort replied with the modest palindrome " Eve."

Then we have Arithmetical Puzzles, an immense class, full of diversity. These range from the puzzle that the algebraist finds to be nothing but a " simple equation," quite easy of direct solution, up to the profoundest problems in the elegant domain of the theory of numbers.

Next we have the Geometrical Puzzle, a favourite and very ancient branch of which is the puzzle in dissection, requiring some plane figure to be cut into a certain number of pieces that will fit together and form another figure. Most of the wire puzzles sold in the streets and toy-shops are concerned with the geometry of position.

But these classes do not nearly embrace all kinds of puzzles even when we allow for those that belong at once to several of the classes. There are many ingenious mechanical puzzles that you cannot classify, as they stand quite alone : there are puzzles in logic, in chess, in draughts, in cards, and in dominoes, while every conjuring trick is nothing but a puzzle, the solution to which the performer tries to keep to himself.

There are puzzles that look easy and are easy, puzzles that look easy and are difficult, puzzles that look difficult and are difficult, and puzzles that look difficult and are easy, and in each class we may of course have degrees of easiness and difficulty. But it does not follow that a puzzle that has conditions that are easily understood by the merest child is in itself easy. Such a puzzle might, however, look simple to the uninformed, and only prove to be a very hard nut to him after he had actually tackled it.

For example, if we write down nineteen ones to form the number

1,111,111,111,111,111,111, and then ask for a number (other than 1 or itself) that will divide it without remainder, the conditions are perfectly simple, but the task is terribly difficult. Nobody in the world knows yet whether that number has a divisor or not. If you can find one, you will have succeeded in doing something that nobody else has ever done.*

The number composed of seventeen ones, 11,111,111,111,111,111, has only these two divisors, 2,071,723 and 5,363,222,357, and their discovery is an exceedingly heavy task. The only number composed only of ones that we know with certainty to have no divisor is 11. Such a number is, of course, called a prime number.

The maxim that there are always a right way and a wrong way of doing anything applies in a very marked degree to the solving of puzzles. Here the wrong way consists in making aimless trials without method, hoping to hit on the answer by accident—a process that generally results in our getting hopelessly entangled in the trap that has been artfully laid for us.

Occasionally, however, a problem is of such a character that, though it may be solved immediately by trial, it is very difficult to do by a process of pure reason. But in most cases the latter method is the only one that gives any real pleasure.

When we sit down to solve a puzzle, the first thing to do is to make sure, as far as we can, that we understand the conditions. For if we do not understand what it is we have to do, we are not very likely to succeed in doing it. We all know the story of the man who was asked the question, " If a herring and a half cost three-halfpence, how much will a dozen herrings cost ? " After several unsuccessful attempts he gave it up, when the propounder explained to him that a dozen herrings would cost a shilling. " Herrings ! " exclaimed the other apologetically ; " I was working it out in haddocks ! "

It sometimes requires more care than the reader might suppose so to word the conditions of a new puzzle that they are at once

* See footnote on page 198.

clear and exact and not so prolix as to destroy all interest in the thing. I remember once propounding a problem that required something to be done in the "fewest possible straight lines," and a person who was either very clever or very foolish (I have never quite determined which) claimed to have solved it in only one straight line, because, as she said, " I have taken care to make all the others crooked ! " Who could have anticipated such a quibble ?

Then if you give a "crossing the river" puzzle, in which people have to be got over in a boat that will only hold a certain number or combination of persons, directly the would-be solver fails to master the difficulty he boldly introduces a rope to pull the boat across. You say that a rope is forbidden ; and he then falls back on the use of a current in the stream. I once thought I had carefully excluded all such tricks in a particular puzzle of this class. But a sapient reader made all the people swim across without using the boat at all ! Of course, some few puzzles are intended to be solved by some trick of this kind ; and if there happens to be no solution without the trick it is perfectly legitimate. We have to use our best judgment as to whether a puzzle contains a catch or not ; but we should never hastily assume it. To quibble over the conditions is the last resort of the defeated would-be solver.

Sometimes people will attempt to bewilder you by curious little twists in the meaning of words. A man recently propounded to me the old familiar problem, " A boy walks round a pole on which is a monkey, but as the boy walks the monkey turns on the pole so as to be always facing him on the opposite side. Does the boy go around the monkey ? " I replied that if he would first give me his definition of " to go around " I would supply him with the answer. Of course, he demurred, so that he might catch me either way. I therefore said that, taking the words in their ordinary and correct meaning, most certainly the boy went around the monkey. As was expected, he retorted that it was not so, because he understood by " going around " a thing that you went in such a way as to see all sides of it. To this I made the obvious reply that consequently a blind man could not go around anything.

He then amended his definition by saying that the actual seeing all sides was not essential, but you went in such a way that, given sight, you could see all sides. Upon which it was suggested that consequently you could not walk around a man who had been shut up in a box! And so on. The whole thing is amusingly stupid, and if at the start you, very properly, decline to admit any but a simple and correct definition of " to go around," there is no puzzle left, and you prevent an idle, and often heated, argument.

When you have grasped your conditions, always see if you cannot simplify them, for a lot of confusion is got rid of in this way. Many people are puzzled over the old question of the man who, while pointing at a portrait, says, " Brothers and sisters have I none, but that man's father is my father's son." What relation did the man in the picture bear to the speaker ? Here you simplify by saying that " my father's son " must be either " myself " or " my brother." But, since the speaker has no brother, it is clearly " myself." The statement simplified is thus nothing more than, " That man's father is myself," and it was obviously his son's portrait. Yet people fight over this question by the hour !

There are mysteries that have never been solved in many branches of Puzzledom. Let us consider a few in the world of numbers— little things the conditions of which a child can understand, though the greatest minds cannot master. Everybody has heard the remark, " It is as hard as squaring a circle," though many people have a very hazy notion of what it means. If you have a circle of given diameter and wish to find the side of a square that shall contain exactly the same area, you are confronted with the problem of squaring the circle. Well, it cannot be done with exactitude (though we can get an answer near enough for all practical purposes), because it is not possible to say in exact numbers what is the ratio of the diameter to the circumference. But it is only in recent times that it has been proved to be impossible, for it is one thing not to be able to perform a certain feat, but quite another to prove that it cannot be done. Only uninstructed cranks now waste their time in trying to square the circle.

Again, we can never measure exactly in numbers the diagonal of a square. If you have a window pane exactly a foot on every side, there is the distance from corner to corner staring you in the face, yet you can never say in exact numbers what is the length of that diagonal. The simple person will at once suggest that we might take our diagonal first, say an exact foot, and then construct our square. Yes, you can do this, but then you can never say exactly what is the length of the side. You can have it which way you like, but you cannot have it both ways.

All my readers know what a magic square is. The numbers 1 to 9 can be arranged in a square of nine cells, so that all the columns and rows and each of the diagonals will add up 15. It is quite easy; and there is only one way of doing it, for we do not count as different the arrangements obtained by merely turning round the square and reflecting it in a mirror. Now if we wish to make a magic square of the 16 numbers, 1 to 16, there are just 880 different ways of doing it, again not counting reversals and reflections. This has been finally proved of recent years. But how many magic squares may be formed with the 25 numbers, 1 to 25, nobody knows, and we shall have to extend our knowledge in certain directions before we can hope to solve the puzzle. But it is surprising to find that exactly 174,240 such squares may be formed of one particular restricted kind only—the bordered square, in which the inner square of nine cells is itself magic. And I have shown how this number may be at once doubled by merely converting every bordered square —by a simple rule—into a non-bordered one.

Then vain attempts have been made to construct a magic square by what is called a " knight's tour " over the chess-board, numbering each square that the knight visits in succession, 1, 2, 3, 4, etc.; and it has been done, with the exception of the two diagonals, which so far have baffled all efforts. But it is not certain that it cannot be done.

Though the contents of the present volume are in the main entirely original, some very few old friends will be found; but these will not, I trust, prove unwelcome in the new dress that they have received. The puzzles are of every degree of difficulty, and so varied in character that perhaps it is not too much to hope that every true puzzle lover will find ample material to interest—and possibly instruct. In some cases I have dealt with the methods of solution at considerable length, but at other times I have reluctantly felt obliged to restrict myself to giving the bare answers. Had the full solutions and proofs been given in the case of every puzzle, either half the problems would have had to be omitted, or the size of the book greatly increased. And the plan that I have adopted has its advantages, for it leaves scope for the mathematical enthusiast to work out his own analysis. Even in those cases where I have given a general formula for the solution of a puzzle, he will find great interest in verifying it for himself.

THE CANTERBURY PUZZLES

A CHANCE-GATHERED company of pilgrims, on their way to the shrine of Saint Thomas à Becket at Canterbury, met at the old Tabard Inn, later called the Talbot, in Southwark, and the host proposed that they should beguile the ride by each telling a tale to his fellow-pilgrims. This we all know was the origin of the immortal *Canterbury Tales* of our great fourteenth-century poet, Geoffrey Chaucer. Unfortunately, the tales were never completed, and perhaps that is why the quaint and curious " Canterbury Puzzles," devised and propounded by the same body of pilgrims, were not also recorded by the poet's pen. This is greatly to be regretted, since Chaucer, who, as Leland tells us, was an " ingenious mathematician " and the author of a learned treatise on the astrolabe, was peculiarly fitted for the propounding of problems. In presenting for the first time some of these old-world posers, I will not stop to explain the singular manner in which they came into my possession, but proceed at once, without unnecessary preamble, to give my readers an opportunity of solving them and testing their quality. There are certainly far more difficult puzzles extant, but difficulty and interest are two qualities of puzzledom that do not necessarily go together.

I.—*The Reve's Puzzle.*

The Reve was a wily man and something of a scholar. **As** Chaucer tells us, " There was no auditor could of him win," and " there could no man bring him in arrear." The poet also noticed that " ever he rode the hindermost of the route." This he did that he might the better, without interruption, work out the fanciful problems and ideas that passed through his active brain. When the

pilgrims were stopping at a wayside tavern, a number of cheeses of varying sizes caught his alert eye ; and calling for four stools, he told the company that he would show them a puzzle of his own that would keep them amused during their rest. He then placed eight cheeses of graduating sizes on one of the end stools, the smallest cheese being at the top, as clearly shown in the illustration. " This is a riddle," quoth he, " that I did once set before my fellow towns- men at Baldeswell, that is in Norfolk, and, by Saint Joce, there was no man among them that could rede it aright. And yet it is withal full easy, for all that I do desire is that, by the moving of one cheese at a time from one stool unto another, ye shall remove all the cheeses to the stool at the other end without ever putting any cheese on one that is smaller than itself. To him that will perform this feat in the least number of moves that be possible will I give a draught of the best that our good host can provide." To solve this puzzle in the fewest possible moves, first with 8, then with 10, and afterwards with 21 cheeses, is an interesting recreation.

2.—*The Pardoner's Puzzle.*

The gentle Pardoner, " that straight was come from the court of Rome," begged to be excused ; but the company would not spare him. " Friends and fellow-pilgrims," said he, " of a truth the riddle that I have made is but a poor thing, but it is the best that

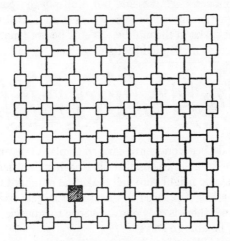

I have been able to devise. Blame my lack of knowledge of such matters if it be not to your liking." But his invention was very well received. He produced the accompanying plan, and said that it represented sixty-four towns through which he had to pass

during some of his pilgrimages, and the lines connecting them were roads. He explained that the puzzle was to start from the large black town and visit all the other towns once, and once only, in fifteen straight pilgrimages. Try to trace the route in fifteen straight lines with your pencil. You may end where you like, but note that the omission of a little road at the bottom is intentional, as it seems that it was impossible to go that way.

3.—*The Miller's Puzzle.*

The Miller next took the company aside and showed them nine sacks of flour that were standing as depicted in the sketch. "Now, hearken, all and some," said he, "while that I do set ye the riddle of the nine sacks of flour. And mark ye, my lords and masters, that there be single sacks on the outside, pairs next unto them, and three together in the middle thereof. By Saint Benedict, it doth so happen that if we do but multiply the pair, 28, by the single one, 7, the answer is 196, which is of a truth the number shown by the sacks in the middle. Yet it be not true that the other pair, 34, when so multiplied by its neighbour, 5, will also make 196.

Wherefore I do beg you, gentle sirs, so to place anew the nine sacks with as little trouble as possible that each pair when thus multiplied by its single neighbour shall make the number in the middle." As the Miller has stipulated in effect that as few bags as possible shall be moved, there is only one answer to this puzzle, which everybody should be able to solve.

4.—*The Knight's Puzzle.*

This worthy man was, as Chaucer tells us, "a very perfect, gentle knight," and " In many a noble army had he been : At mortal battles had he been fifteen." His shield, as he is seen showing it to the company at the "Tabard" in the illustration, was, in the peculiar language of the heralds, "argent, semée of roses, gules," which means that on a white ground red roses were

scattered or strewn, as seed is sown by the hand. When this knight was called on to propound a puzzle, he said to the company, "This riddle a wight did ask of me when that I fought with the lord of Palatine against the heathen in Turkey. In thy hand take a piece of chalk and learn how many perfect squares thou canst make with one of the eighty-seven roses at each corner thereof." The reader may find it an interesting problem to count the number of squares that may be formed on the shield by uniting four roses.

5.—*The Wife of Bath's Riddles.*

The frolicsome Wife of Bath, when called upon to favour the company, protested that she had no aptitude for such things, but that her fourth husband had had a liking for them, and she remembered one of his riddles that might be new to her fellow pilgrims: " Why is a bung that hath been made fast in a barrel like unto another bung that is just falling out of a barrel ? " As the company promptly answered this easy conundrum, the lady went on to say that when she was one day seated sewing in her private chamber her son entered. " Upon receiving," saith she, " the parental command, ' Depart, my son, and do not disturb me ! ' he did reply, ' I am, of a truth, thy son ; but thou art not my mother, and until thou hast shown me how this may be I shall not go forth.' " This perplexed the company a good deal, but it is not likely to give the reader much difficulty.

6.—*The Host's Puzzle.*

Perhaps no puzzle of the whole collection caused more jollity or was found more entertaining than that produced by the Host of the "Tabard," who accompanied the party all the way. He called the pilgrims together and spoke as follows : "My merry masters all, now that it be my turn to give your brains a twist, I will show ye a little piece of craft that will try your wits to their full bent. And yet methinks it is but a simple matter when the doing of it is made clear. Here be a cask of fine London ale, and in my hands do I hold two measures—one of five pints, and the other of three pints. Pray show how it is possible for me to put a true pint into each of the measures." Of course, no other vessel or article is to be used, and no marking of the measures is allowed. It is a knotty little problem and a fascinating one. A good many persons to-day will find it by no means an easy task. Yet it can be done.

7.—*The Clerk of Oxenford's Puzzle.*

The silent and thoughtful Clerk of Oxenford, of whom it is recorded that " Every farthing that his friends e'er lent, In books and learning was it always spent," was prevailed upon to give his

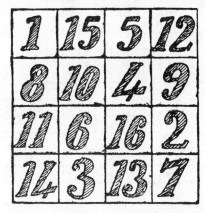

companions a puzzle. He said, " Ofttimes of late have I given much thought to the study of those strange talismans to ward off the plague and such evils that are yclept magic squares, and the secret of such things is very deep and the number of such squares truly great. But the small riddle that I did make yester eve for the purpose of this company is not so hard that any may not find it out with a little patience." He then produced the square shown in the illustration and said that it was desired so to cut it into four pieces (by cuts along the lines) that they would fit together again and form a perfect magic square, in which the four columns, the four rows, and the two long diagonals should add up 34. It will be found that this is a just sufficiently easy puzzle for most people's tastes.

8.—*The Tapiser's Puzzle.*

Then came forward the Tapiser, who was, of course, a maker of tapestry, and must not be confounded with a tapster, who draws and sells ale.

He produced a beautiful piece of tapestry, worked in a simple chequered pattern, as shown in the diagram. " This piece of

tapestry, sirs," quoth he, " hath one hundred and sixty-nine small squares, and I do desire you to tell me the manner of cutting the tapestry into three pieces that shall fit together and make one whole piece in shape of a perfect square.

" Moreover, since there be divers ways of so doing, I do wish to know that way wherein two of the pieces shall together contain as much as possible of the rich fabric." It is clear that the Tapiser intended the cuts to be made along the lines dividing the squares only, and, as the material was not both sides alike, no piece may be reversed, but care must be observed that the chequered pattern matches properly.

9.—The Carpenter's Puzzle.

The Carpenter produced the carved wooden pillar that he is seen holding in the illustration, wherein the knight is propounding his knotty problem to the goodly company (No. 4), and spoke as follows : " There dwelleth in the city of London a certain scholar that is learned in astrology and other strange arts. Some few days gone he did bring unto me a piece of wood that had three feet in length, one foot in breadth and one foot in depth, and did desire that it be carved and made into the pillar that you do now behold. Also did he promise certain payment for every cubic inch of wood cut away by the carving thereof.

" Now I did at first weigh the block, and found it truly to contain thirty pounds, whereas the pillar doth now weigh but twenty pounds. Of a truth I have therefore cut away one cubic foot (which is to say one-third) of the three cubic feet of the block; but this scholar withal doth hold that payment may not thus be fairly made by weight, since the heart of the block may be heavier, or perchance may be more light, than the outside. How then may I with ease satisfy the scholar as to the quantity of wood that hath been cut away ? " This at first sight looks a difficult question, but it is so absurdly simple that the method employed by the carpenter should be known to everybody to-day, for it is a very useful little " wrinkle."

10.—The Puzzle of the Squire's Yeoman.

Chaucer says of the Squire's Yeoman, who formed one of his party of pilgrims, " A forester was he truly as I guess," and tells us that " His arrows drooped not with feathers low, And in his hand he bare a mighty bow." When a halt was made one day at a wayside inn, bearing the old sign of the " Chequers," this yeoman consented to give the company an exhibition of his skill. Selecting nine good arrows, he said, " Mark ye, good sirs, how that I shall shoot these nine arrows in such manner that each of them shall lodge in the middle of one of the squares that be upon the sign of the ' Chequers,' and yet of a truth shall no arrow be in line with any other arrow." The diagram will show exactly how he did this, and no two arrows will be found in line, horizontally, vertically,

or diagonally. Then the Yeoman said : " Here then is a riddle for ye. Remove three of the arrows each to one of its neighbouring squares, so that the nine shall yet be so placed that none thereof may be in line with another." By a " neighbouring square " is meant one that adjoins, either laterally or diagonally.

11.—*The Nun's Puzzle.*

" I trow there be not one among ye," quoth the Nun, on a later occasion, " that doth not know that many monks do oft pass the time in play at certain games, albeit they be not lawful for them. These games, such as cards and the game of chess, do they cunningly hide from the abbot's eye by putting them away in holes that they have cut out of the very hearts of great books that be upon their shelves. Shall the nun therefore be greatly blamed if she do likewise ? I will show a little riddle game that we do sometimes play among ourselves when the good abbess doth hap to be away."

The Nun then produced the eighteen cards that are shown in the illustration. She explained that the puzzle was so to arrange the cards in a pack, that by placing the uppermost one on the table, placing the next one at the bottom of the pack, the next one on the

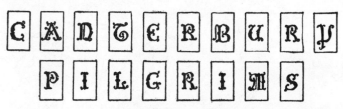

table, the next at the bottom of the pack, and so on, until all are on the table, the eighteen cards shall then read " CANTERBURY PILGRIMS." Of course each card must be placed on the table to the immediate right of the one that preceded it. It is easy enough if you work backwards, but the reader should try to arrive at the required order without doing this, or using any actual cards.

12.—The Merchant's Puzzle.

Of the Merchant the poet writes, " Forsooth he was a worthy man withal." He was thoughtful, full of schemes, and a good manipulator of figures. " His reasons spake he eke full solemnly, Sounding alway the increase of his winning." One morning, when they were on the road, the Knight and the Squire, who were riding beside him, reminded the Merchant that he had not yet propounded the puzzle that he owed the company. He thereupon said, " Be it so ? Here then is a riddle in numbers that I will set before this merry company when next we do make a halt. There be thirty of us in all riding over the common this morn. Truly we may ride one and one, in what they do call the single file, or two and two, or three and three, or five and five, or six and six, or ten and ten, or fifteen and fifteen, or all thirty in a row. In no other way may we ride so that there be no lack of equal numbers in the rows. Now, a party of pilgrims were able thus to ride in as many as sixty-

four different ways. Prithee tell me how many there must perforce have been in the company." The Merchant clearly required the smallest number of persons that could so ride in the sixty-four ways.

13.—*The Man of Law's Puzzle.*

The Sergeant of the Law was " full rich of excellence. Discreet he was, and of great reverence." He was a very busy man, but, like many of us to-day, " he seemed busier than he was." He was talking one evening of prisons and prisoners, and at length made the following remarks : " And that which I have been saying doth forsooth call to my mind that this morn I bethought me of a riddle that I will now put forth." He then produced a slip of vellum, on which was drawn the curious plan that is now given. "Here," saith he, "be nine dungeons, with a prisoner in every dungeon save one, which is empty. These prisoners be numbered in order, 7, 5, 6, 8, 2, 1, 4, 3, and I desire to know how they can, in as few moves as possible, put themselves in the order 1, 2, 3, 4, 5, 6, 7, 8. One prisoner may move at a time along the passage to the dungeon that doth happen to be empty, but never, on pain of death, may

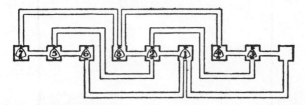

two men be in any dungeon at the same time. How may it be done ?" If the reader makes a rough plan on a sheet of paper and uses numbered counters, he will find it an interesting pastime to arrange the prisoners in the fewest possible moves. As there is never more than one vacant dungeon at a time to be moved into, the moves may be recorded in this simple way: 3—2—1—6, and so on.

14.—*The Weaver's Puzzle.*

When the Weaver brought out a square piece of beautiful cloth, daintily embroidered with lions and castles, as depicted in the illustration, the pilgrims disputed among themselves as to the meaning of these ornaments. The Knight, however, who was skilled in heraldry, explained that they were probably derived from the lions and castles borne in the arms of Ferdinand III., the King of Castile and Leon, whose daughter was the first wife of our Edward I. In this he was undoubtedly correct. The puzzle that the Weaver proposed was this. "Let us, for the nonce, see," saith he, "if there be any of the company that can show how this piece of cloth may be cut into four several pieces, each of the same size and shape, and each piece bearing a lion and a castle." It is not

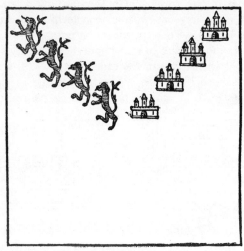

recorded that anybody mastered this puzzle, though it is quite possible of solution in a satisfactory manner. No cut may pass through any part of a lion or a castle.

15.—*The Cook's Puzzle.*

We find that there was a cook among the company; and his services were no doubt at times in great request, " For he could roast and seethe, and broil and fry, And make a mortress and well bake a pie." One night when the pilgrims were seated at a country hostelry, about to begin their repast, the cook presented himself at the head of the table that was presided over by the Franklin, and said, "Listen awhile, my masters, while that I do ask ye a riddle, and by Saint Moden it is one that I cannot answer myself withal. There be eleven pilgrims seated at this board on which is set a warden pie and a venison pasty, each of which may truly be divided into four parts and no more. Now, mark ye, five out of the eleven pilgrims can eat the pie, but will not touch the pasty, while four will eat the pasty but turn away from the pie. Moreover, the two that do remain be able and willing to eat of either. By my hali-dame, is there any that can tell me in how many different ways the good Franklin may choose whom he will serve?" I will just

caution the reader that if he is not careful he will find, when he sees the answer, that he has made a mistake of forty, as all the company did, with the exception of the Clerk of Oxenford, who got it right by accident, through putting down a wrong figure.

Strange to say, while the company perplexed their wits about this riddle the cook played upon them a merry jest. In the midst of their deep thinking and hot dispute what should the cunning knave do but stealthily take away both the pie and the pasty. Then, when hunger made them desire to go on with the repast, finding there was nought upon the table, they called clamorously for the cook.

" My masters," he explained, " seeing you were so deep set in the riddle, I did take them to the next room, where others did eat them with relish ere they had grown cold. There be excellent bread and cheese in the pantry."

16.—*The Sompnour's Puzzle.*

The Sompnour, or Summoner, who, according to Chaucer, joined the party of pilgrims, was an officer whose duty was to summon delinquents to appear in ecclesiastical courts. In later times he became known as the apparitor. Our particular individual was a somewhat quaint though worthy man. " He was

a gentle hireling and a kind ; A better fellow should a man not find." In order that the reader may understand his appearance in the picture, it must be explained that his peculiar headgear is duly recorded by the poet. " A garland had he set upon his head, As great as if it were for an ale-stake."

One evening ten of the company stopped at a village inn and

requested to be put up for the night, but mine host could only accommodate five of them. The Sompnour suggested that they should draw lots, and as he had had experience in such matters in the summoning of juries and in other ways, he arranged the company in a circle and proposed a " count out." Being of a chivalrous nature, his little plot was so to arrange that the men should all fall out and leave the ladies in possession. He therefore gave the Wife of Bath a number and directed her to count round and round the circle, in a clockwise direction, and the person on whom that number fell was immediately to step out of the ring. The count then began afresh at the next person. But the lady misunderstood her instructions, and selected in mistake the number eleven and started the count at herself. As will be found, this resulted in all the women falling out in turn instead of the men, for every eleventh person withdrawn from the circle is a lady.

" Of a truth it was no fault of mine," said the Sompnour next day to the company, " and herein is methinks a riddle. Can any tell me what number the good Wife should have used withal, and at which pilgrim she should have begun her count so that no other than the five men should have been counted out ? " Of course, the point is to find the smallest number that will have the desired effect.

17.—*The Monk's Puzzle.*

The Monk that went with the party was a great lover of sport. " Greyhounds he had as swift as fowl of flight : Of riding and of hunting for the hare Was all his love, for no cost would he spare." One day he addressed the pilgrims as follows :—

" There is a little matter that hath at times perplexed me greatly, though certes it is of no great weight; yet may it serve to try the wits of some that be cunning in such things. Nine kennels have I for the use of my dogs, and they be put in the form of a square; though the one in the middle I do never use, it not being of a useful nature. Now the riddle is to find in how many different ways I may place my dogs in all or any of the outside kennels so that the number of dogs on every side of the square may be just ten." The small diagrams show four ways of doing it, and though the fourth

way is merely a reversal of the third, it counts as different. Any kennels may be left empty. This puzzle was evidently a variation of the ancient one of the Abbess and her Nuns.

18.—*The Shipman's Puzzle.*

Of this person we are told, " He knew well all the havens, as they were, From Gothland to the Cape of Finisterre, And every creek in Brittany and Spain : His barque yclepéd was the *Magdalen.*" The strange puzzle in navigation that he propounded was as follows.

" Here be a chart," quoth the Shipman, " of five islands, with the inhabitants of which I do trade. In each year my good ship doth sail over every one of the ten courses depicted thereon, but never may she pass along the same course twice in any year. Is there any among the company who can tell me in how many different ways I may direct the *Magdalen's* ten yearly voyages always setting out from the same island ? "

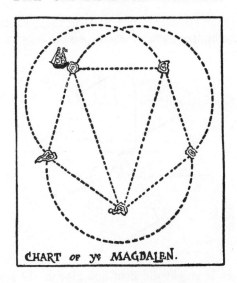

CHART OF Yᵉ MAGDALEN.

19.—*The Puzzle of the Prioress.*

The Prioress, who went by the name of Eglantine, is best remembered on account of Chaucer's remark, " And French she spake full fair and properly, After the school of Stratford-atté-Bow, For French of Paris was to her unknow." But our puzzle has to do less with her character and education than with her dress. " And thereon hung a brooch of gold full sheen, On which was written first a crownéd A." It is with the brooch that we are concerned, for when asked to give a puzzle she showed this jewel to the company and said : " A learned man from Normandy did once give me this brooch as a charm, saying strange and mystic things anent it, how that it hath an affinity for the square, and such other wise words that were too subtle for me. But the good Abbot of Chertsey did once tell me that the cross may be so cunningly cut into four pieces that they will join and make a perfect square; though on my faith I know not the manner of doing it."

It is recorded that " the pilgrims did find no answer to the riddle, and the Clerk of Oxenford thought that the Prioress had been deceived in the matter thereof; whereupon the lady was sore vexed,

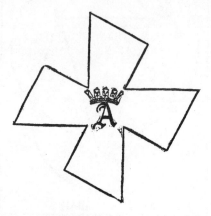

though the gentle knight did flout and gibe at the poor clerk because of his lack of understanding over other of the riddles, which did fill him with shame and make merry the company."

20.—*The Puzzle of the Doctor of Physic.*

This Doctor, learned though he was, for " In all this world to him there was none like To speak of physic and of surgery," and " He knew the cause of every malady," yet was he not indifferent to the more material side of life. " Gold in physic is a cordial; Therefore he loved gold in special." The problem that the Doctor propounded to the assembled pilgrims was this. He produced two spherical phials, as shown in our illustration, and pointed out that one phial was exactly a foot in circumference, and the other two feet in circumference.

" I do wish," said the Doctor, addressing the company, " to have the exact measures of two other phials, of a like shape but different in size, that may together contain just as much liquid as is contained by these two." To find exact dimensions in the

smallest possible numbers is one of the toughest nuts I have attempted. Of course the thickness of the glass, and the neck and base, are to be ignored.

21.—*The Ploughman's Puzzle.*

The Ploughman—of whom Chaucer remarked, " A worker true

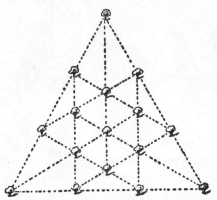

and very good was he, Living in perfect peace and charity "—
protested that riddles were not for simple minds like his, but he

would show the good pilgrims, if they willed it, one that he had frequently heard certain clever folk in his own neighbourhood discuss. "The lord of the manor in the part of Sussex whence I come hath a plantation of sixteen fair oak trees, and they be so set out that they make twelve rows with four trees in every row. Once on a time a man of deep learning, who happened to be travelling in those parts, did say that the sixteen trees might have been so planted that they would make so many as fifteen straight rows, with four trees in every row thereof. Can ye show me how this might be ? Many have doubted that 'twere possible to be done." The illustration shows one of many ways of forming the twelve rows. How can we make fifteen ?

22.—*The Franklin's Puzzle.*

" A Franklin was in this company ; White was his beard as is the daisy." We are told by Chaucer that he was a great householder and an epicure. " Without baked meat never was his house. Of fish and flesh, and that so plenteous, It snowed in his

house of meat and drink, Of every dainty that men could bethink." He was a hospitable and generous man. " His table dormant in his hall alway Stood ready covered all throughout the day." At the repasts of the Pilgrims he usually presided at one of the tables, as we found him doing on the occasion when the cook propounded his problem of the two pies.

One day, at an inn just outside Canterbury, the company called on him to produce the puzzle required of him; whereupon he placed on the table sixteen bottles numbered 1, 2, 3, up to 15, with the last one marked 0. "Now, my masters," quoth he, "it will be fresh in your memories how that the good Clerk of Oxenford did show us a riddle touching what hath been called the magic square. Of a truth will I set before ye another that may seem to be somewhat of a like kind, albeit there be little in common betwixt them. Here be set out sixteen bottles in form of a square, and I pray you so place them afresh that they shall form a magic square, adding up to thirty in all the ten straight ways. But mark well that ye may not remove more than ten of the bottles from their present places, for therein layeth the subtlety of the riddle." This is a little puzzle that may be conveniently tried with sixteen numbered counters.

23.—*The Squire's Puzzle.*

The young Squire, twenty years of age, was the son of the Knight that accompanied him on the historic pilgrimage. He was undoubtedly what in later times we should call a dandy, for, "Embroideréd was he as is a mead, All full of fresh flowers, white and red. Singing he was or fluting all the day, He was as fresh as is the month of May." As will be seen in the illustration to No. 26, while the Haberdasher was propounding his problem of the triangle, this young Squire was standing in the background making a drawing of some kind; for "He could songs make and well indite, Joust and eke dance, and well portray and write."

The Knight turned to him after a while and said, "My son, what is it over which thou dost take so great pains withal?" and the Squire answered, "I have bethought me how I might portray in one only stroke a picture of our late sovereign lord King Edward the Third, who hath been dead these ten years. 'Tis a riddle to find where the stroke doth begin and where it doth also end. To him who first shall show it unto me will I give the portraiture."

I am able to present a facsimile of the original drawing, which

was won by the Man of Law. It may be here remarked that the pilgrimage set out from Southwark on 17th April 1387, and Edward the Third died in 1377.

24.—*The Friar's Puzzle.*

The Friar was a merry fellow, with a sweet tongue and twinkling eyes. " Courteous he was and lowly of service. There was a man nowhere so virtuous." Yet he was " the best beggar in all his house," and gave reasons why " Therefore, instead of weeping and much prayer, Men must give silver to the needy friar." He went by the name of Hubert. One day he produced four money bags and spoke as follows : " If the needy friar doth receive in alms five hundred silver pennies, prithee tell in how many different

ways they may be placed in the four bags." The good man explained that order made no difference (so that the distribution 50,
100, 150, 200 would be the same as 100, 50, 200, 150, or 200, 50,
100, 150), and one, two, or three bags may at any time be empty.

25.—*The Parson's Puzzle.*

The Parson was a really devout and good man. " A better
priest I trow there nowhere is." His virtues and charity made
him beloved by all his flock, to whom he presented his teaching
with patience and simplicity; "but first he followed it himself."
Now, Chaucer is careful to tell us that " Wide was his parish, and

houses far asunder, But he neglected nought for rain or thunder;"
and it is with his parochial visitations that the Parson's puzzle
actually dealt. He produced a plan of part of his parish, through

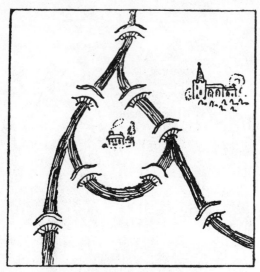

which a small river ran that joined the sea some hundreds of miles
to the south. I give a facsimile of the plan.

"Here, my worthy Pilgrims, is a strange riddle," quoth the
Parson. "Behold how at the branching of the river is an island.
Upon this island doth stand my own poor parsonage, and ye may
all see the whereabouts of the village church. Mark ye, also, that
there be eight bridges and no more over the river in my parish.
On my way to church it is my wont to visit sundry of my flock, and
in the doing thereof I do pass over every one of the eight bridges
once and no more. Can any of ye find the path, after this manner,
from the house to the church, without going out of the parish?
Nay, nay, my friends, I do never cross the river in any boat, neither
by swimming nor wading, nor do I go underground like unto the
mole, nor fly in the air as doth the eagle; but only pass over by the

bridges." There is a way in which the Parson might have made this curious journey. Can the reader discover it? At first it seems impossible, but the conditions offer a loophole.

26.—*The Haberdasher's Puzzle.*

Many attempts were made to induce the Haberdasher, who was of the party, to propound a puzzle of some kind, but for a long time without success. At last, at one of the Pilgrims' stopping-places, he said that he would show them something that

would "put their brains into a twist like unto a bell-rope." As a matter of fact, he was really playing off a practical joke on the company, for he was quite ignorant of any answer to the puzzle that he set them. He produced a piece of cloth in the shape of a perfect equilateral triangle, as shown in the illustration, and said, " Be there any among ye full wise in the true cutting of cloth ? I trow not. Every man to his trade, and the scholar may learn from the varlet and the wise man from the fool. Show me, then, if ye can, in what manner this piece of cloth may be cut into four several pieces that may be put together to make a perfect square."

Now some of the more learned of the company found a way of doing it in five pieces, but not in four. But when they pressed the Haberdasher for the correct answer he was forced to admit, after much beating about the bush, that he knew no way of doing it in any number of pieces. " By Saint Francis," saith he, " any knave can make a riddle methinks, but it is for them that may to rede it aright." For this he narrowly escaped a sound beating. But the curious point of the puzzle is that I have found that the feat may really be performed in so few as four pieces, and without turning over any piece when placing them together. The method of doing this is subtle, but I think the reader will find the problem a most interesting one.

27.—*The Dyer's Puzzle.*

One of the pilgrims was a Dyer, but Chaucer tells us nothing about him, the Tales being incomplete. Time after time the company had pressed this individual to produce a puzzle of some kind, but without effect. The poor fellow tried his best to follow the examples of his friends the Tapiser, the Weaver, and the Haberdasher; but the necessary idea would not come, rack his brains as he would. All things, however, come to those who wait—and persevere—and one morning he announced, in a state of considerable excitement, that he had a poser to set before them. He brought out a square piece of silk on which were embroidered a number of fleurs-de-lys in rows, as shown in our illustration.

" Lordings," said the Dyer, " hearken anon unto my riddle. Since I was awakened at dawn by the crowing of cocks—for which din may our host never thrive—I have sought an answer thereto, but by St. Bernard I have found it not. There be sixty-and-four flowers-de-luce, and the riddle is to show how I may remove six of these so that there may yet be an even number of the flowers in every row and every column."

The Dyer was abashed when every one of the company showed

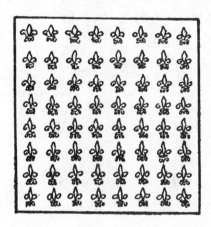

without any difficulty whatever, and each in a different way, how this might be done. But the good Clerk of Oxenford was seen to whisper something to the Dyer, who added, "Hold, my masters! What I have said is not all. Ye must find in how many different ways it may be done!" All agreed that this was quite another matter. And only a few of the company got the right answer.

28.—*The Great Dispute between the Friar and the Sompnour.*

Chaucer records the painful fact that the harmony of the pilgrimage was broken on occasions by the quarrels between the Friar and the Sompnour. At one stage the latter threatened that ere they reached Sittingbourne he would make the Friar's "heart for to mourn;" but the worthy Host intervened and patched up a temporary peace. Unfortunately trouble broke out again over a very curious dispute in this way.

At one point of the journey the road lay along two sides of a square field, and some of the pilgrims persisted, in spite of trespass, in cutting across from corner to corner, as they are seen to be doing in the illustration. Now, the Friar startled the company by stating that there was no need for the trespass, since one way was exactly the same distance as the other! "On my faith, then," exclaimed the Sompnour, "thou art a very fool!" "Nay," replied the Friar, "if the company will but listen with patience, I shall presently show how that thou art the fool, for thou hast not wit enough in thy poor brain to prove that the diagonal of any square is less than two of the sides."

If the reader will refer to the diagrams that we have given, he will be able to follow the Friar's argument. If we suppose the side of the field to be 100 yards, then the distance along the two sides, A to B, and B to C, is 200 yards. He undertook to prove that the diagonal distance direct from A to C is also 200 yards. Now, if we take the diagonal path shown in Fig. 1, it is evident that we go the same distance, for every one of the eight straight portions of this path measures exactly 25 yards. Similarly in Fig. 2, the zigzag contains ten straight portions, each 20 yards long: that path is also the same length—200 yards. No matter how many steps we make in our zigzag path, the result is most certainly

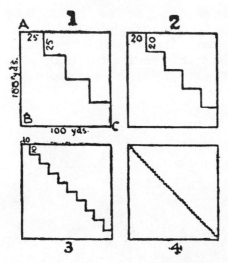

always the same. Thus, in Fig. 3 the steps are very small, yet the distance must be 200 yards; as is also the case in Fig. 4, and would yet be if we needed a microscope to detect the steps. In this way, the Friar argued, we may go on straightening out that zigzag path until we ultimately reach a perfectly straight line, and it therefore follows that the diagonal of a square is of exactly the same length as two of the sides.

Now, in the face of it, this must be wrong; and it is in fact absurdly so, as we can at once prove by actual measurement if we

have any doubt.   Yet the Sompnour could not for the life of him
point out the fallacy, and so upset the Friar's reasoning.   It was
this that so exasperated him, and consequently, like many of us
to-day when we get entangled in an argument, he utterly lost his
temper and resorted to abuse.   In fact, if some of the other pilgrims had not interposed the two would have undoubtedly come
to blows.   The reader will perhaps at once see the flaw in the
Friar's argument.

29.—*Chaucer's Puzzle.*

Chaucer himself accompanied the pilgrims.   Being a mathematician and a man of a thoughtful habit, the Host made fun of him,
he tells us, saying, " Thou lookest as thou wouldst find a hare,
For ever on the ground I see thee stare."   The poet replied to the
request for a tale by launching into a long-spun-out and ridiculous

poem, intended to ridicule the popular romances of the day, after
twenty-two stanzas of which the company refused to hear any
more, and induced him to start another tale in prose.   It is an
interesting fact that in the " Parson's Prologue " Chaucer actually

introduces a little astronomical problem. In modern English this reads somewhat as follows :—

" The sun from the south line was descended so low that it was not to my sight more than twenty-nine degrees. I calculate that it was four o'clock, for, assuming my height to be six feet, my shadow was eleven feet, a little more or less. At the same moment the moon's altitude (she being in mid-Libra) was steadily increasing as we entered at the west end of the village." A correspondent has taken the trouble to work this out, and finds that the local time was 3.58 p.m., correct to a minute, and that the day of the year was the 22nd or 23rd of April, modern style. This speaks well for Chaucer's accuracy, for the first line of the Tales tells us that the pilgrimage was in April—they are supposed to have set out on 17th April 1387, as stated in No. 23.

Though Chaucer made this little puzzle and recorded it for the interest of his readers, he did not venture to propound it to his fellow-pilgrims. The puzzle that he gave them was of a simpler kind altogether : it may be called a geographical one. " When, in the year 1372, I did go into Italy as the envoy of our sovereign lord King Edward the Third, and while there did visit Francesco Petrarch, that learned poet did take me to the top of a certain mountain in his country. Of a truth, as he did show me, a mug will hold less liquor at the top of this mountain than in the valley beneath. Prythee tell me what mountain this may be that has so strange a property withal." A very elementary knowledge of geography will suffice for arriving at the correct answer.

30.—*The Puzzle of the Canon's Yeoman.*

This person joined the party on the road. " ' God save,' quoth he, ' this jolly company ! Fast have I ridden,' saith he, ' for your sake, Because I would I might you overtake, To ride among this merry company.' " Of course, he was asked to entertain the pilgrims with a puzzle, and the one he propounded was the following. He showed them the diamond-shaped arrangement of letters presented in the accompanying illustration, and said, " I do call it the rat-catcher's riddle. In how many different ways canst thou read the words, ' Was it a rat I saw ? ' " You

may go in any direction backwards and forwards, upwards or downwards, only the successive letters in any reading must always adjoin one another.

31.—*The Manciple's Puzzle.*

The Manciple was an officer who had the care of buying victuals for an Inn of Court—like the Temple. The particular individual who accompanied the party was a wily man who had more than thirty masters, and made fools of them all. Yet he was a man " whom purchasers might take as an example How to be wise in buying of their victual."

It happened that at a certain stage of the journey the Miller and the Weaver sat down to a light repast. The Miller produced five loaves and the Weaver three. The Manciple coming upon the scene asked permission to eat with them, to which they agreed. When the Manciple had fed he laid down eight pieces of money and said with a sly smile, " Settle betwixt yourselves how the money shall be fairly divided. 'Tis a riddle for thy wits."

A discussion followed, and many of the pilgrims joined in it. The Reve and the Sompnour held that the Miller should receive five pieces and the Weaver three, the simple Ploughman was ridiculed for suggesting that the Miller should receive seven and the Weaver only one, while the Carpenter, the Monk, and the Cook

insisted that the money should be divided equally between the two men. Various other opinions were urged with considerable vigour, until it was finally decided that the Manciple, as an expert in such matters, should himself settle the point. His decision was quite correct. What was it ? Of course, all three are supposed to have eaten equal shares of the bread.

EVERYBODY that has heard of Solvamhall Castle, and of the quaint customs and ceremonies that obtained there in the olden times, is familiar with the fact that Sir Hugh de Fortibus was a lover of all kinds of puzzles and enigmas. Sir Robert de Riddlesdale himself declared on one occasion, " By the bones of Saint Jingo, this Sir Hugh hath a sharp wit. Certes, I wot not the riddle that he may not rede withal." It is, therefore, a source of particular satisfaction that the recent discovery of some ancient rolls and documents relating mainly to the family of De Fortibus enables me to place before my readers a few of the posers that racked people's brains in the good old days. The selection has been made to suit all tastes, and while the majority will be found sufficiently easy to interest those who like a puzzle that *is* a puzzle, but well within the scope of all, two that I have included may perhaps be found worthy of engaging the attention of the more advanced student of these things.

32.—*The Game of Bandy-Ball.*

Bandy-ball, cambuc, or goff (the game so well known to-day by the name of golf), is of great antiquity, and was a special favourite at Solvamhall Castle. Sir Hugh de Fortibus was himself a master of the game, and he once proposed this question.

They had nine holes, 300, 250, 200, 325, 275, 350, 225, 375, and 400 yards apart. If a man could always strike the ball in a perfectly straight line and send it exactly one of two distances, so that it would either go towards the hole, pass over it, or drop into it, what would the two distances be that would carry him in the least number of strokes round the whole course ?

" Beshrew me," Sir Hugh would say, " if I know any who could do it in this perfect way ; albeit, the point is a pretty one."

Two very good distances are 125 and 75, which carry you round in 28 strokes, but this is not the correct answer. Can the reader get round in fewer strokes with two other distances ?

33.—*Tilting at the Ring.*

Another favourite sport at the castle was tilting at the ring. A horizontal bar was fixed in a post, and at the end of a hanging supporter was placed a circular ring, as shown in the above illustrated title. By raising or lowering the bar the ring could be adjusted to the proper height—generally about the level of the left eyebrow of the horseman. The object was to ride swiftly some eighty paces and run the lance through the ring, which was easily detached, and remained on the lance as the property of the skilful winner. It was a very difficult feat, and men were not unnaturally proud of the rings they had succeeded in capturing.

At one tournament at the castle Henry de Gournay beat Stephen Malet by six rings. Each had his rings made into a chain—De Gournay's chain being exactly sixteen inches in length, and Malet's six inches. Now, as the rings were all of the same size and made of metal half an inch thick, the little puzzle proposed by Sir Hugh was to discover just how many rings each man had won.

34.—*The Noble Demoiselle.*

Seated one night in the hall of the castle, Sir Hugh desired the company to fill their cups and listen while he told the tale of his adventure as a youth in rescuing from captivity a noble demoiselle who was languishing in the dungeon of the castle belonging to his father's greatest enemy. The story was a thrilling one, and when he related the final escape from all the dangers and horrors of the great Death's-head Dungeon with the fair but unconscious maiden in his arms, all exclaimed, " 'Twas marvellous valiant!" But Sir Hugh said, " I would never have turned from my purpose, not even to save my body from the bernicles."

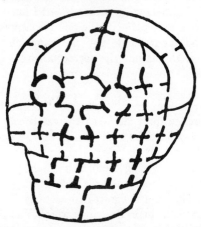

Sir Hugh then produced a plan of the thirty-five cells in the dungeon and asked his companions to discover the particular cell that the demoiselle occupied. He said that if you started at one of the outside cells and passed through every doorway once, and once only, you were bound to end at the cell that was sought. Can you find the cell? Unless you start at the correct outside cell it is impossible to pass through all the doorways once and once only. Try tracing out the route with your pencil.

35.—The Archery Butt.

The butt or target used in archery at Solvamhall was not marked out in concentric rings as at the present day, but was prepared in fanciful designs. In the illustration is shown a numbered target prepared by Sir Hugh himself. It is something of a curiosity, because it will be found that he has so cleverly arranged the numbers that every one of the twelve lines of three adds up to exactly twenty-two.

One day, when the archers were a little tired of their sport, Sir Hugh de Fortibus said, "What ho, merry archers! Of a truth it is said that a fool's bolt is soon shot, but, by my faith, I know

not any man among you who shall do that which I will now put forth. Let these numbers that are upon the butt be set down afresh, so that the twelve lines thereof shall make twenty and three instead of twenty and two."

To rearrange the numbers one to nineteen so that all the twelve lines shall add up to twenty-three will be found a fascinating puzzle. Half the lines are, of course, on the sides, and the others radiate from the centre.

36.—*The Donjon Keep Window.*

On one occasion Sir Hugh greatly perplexed his chief builder. He took this worthy man to the walls of the donjon keep and pointed to a window there.

" Methinks," said he, " yon window is square, and measures, on the inside, one foot every way, and is divided by the narrow bars into four lights, measuring half a foot on every side."

" Of a truth that is so, Sir Hugh."

" Then I desire that another window be made higher up whose

four sides shall also be each one foot, but it shall be divided by bars into eight lights, whose sides shall be all equal."

" Truly, Sir Hugh," said the bewildered chief builder, " I know not how it may be done."

" By my halidame ! " exclaimed De Fortibus in pretended rage, " let it be done forthwith. I trow thou art but a sorry craftsman if thou canst not, forsooth, set such a window in a keep wall."

It will be noticed that Sir Hugh ignores the thickness of the bars.

37.—*The Crescent and the Cross.*

When Sir Hugh's kinsman, Sir John de Collingham, came back from the Holy Land, he brought with him a flag bearing the sign of a crescent, as shown in the illustration. It was noticed that De Fortibus spent much time in examining this crescent and comparing it with the cross borne by the Crusaders on their own banners. One day, in the presence of a goodly company, he made the following striking announcement :—

" I have thought much of late, friends and masters, of the conversion of the crescent to the cross, and this has led me to the

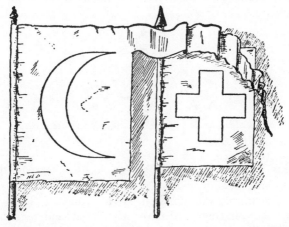

finding of matters at which I marvel greatly, for that which I shall now make known is mystical and deep. Truly it was shown to me in a dream that this crescent of the enemy may be exactly converted into the cross of our own banner. Herein is a sign that bodes good for our wars in the Holy Land."

Sir Hugh de Fortibus then explained that the crescent in one banner might be cut into pieces that would exactly form the perfect cross in the other. It is certainly rather curious ; and I show how the conversion from crescent to cross may be made in ten pieces, using every part of the crescent. The flag was alike on both sides, so pieces may be turned over where required.

38.—*The Amulet.*

A strange man was one day found loitering in the courtyard of the castle, and the retainers, noticing that his speech had a foreign accent, suspected him of being a spy. So the fellow was brought before Sir Hugh, who could make nothing of him. He ordered the varlet to be removed and examined, in order to discover whether any secret letters were concealed about him. All they found was a piece of parchment securely suspended from the neck, bearing this mysterious inscription :—

To-day we know that Abracadabra was the supreme deity of the Assyrians, and this curious arrangement of the letters of the word was commonly worn in Europe as an amulet or charm against diseases. But Sir Hugh had never heard of it, and, regarding the document rather seriously, he sent for a learned priest.

" I pray you, Sir Clerk," said he, " show me the true intent of this strange writing."

" Sir Hugh," replied the holy man, after he had spoken in a foreign tongue with the stranger, " it is but an amulet that this poor wight doth wear upon his breast to ward off the ague, the toothache, and such other afflictions of the body."

" Then give the varlet food and raiment and set him on his way," said Sir Hugh. " Meanwhile, Sir Clerk, canst thou tell me in

how many ways this word ' Abracadabra ' may be read on the
amulet, always starting from the A at the top thereof ? "

Place your pencil on the A at the top and count in how many
different ways you can trace out the word downwards, always
passing from a letter to an adjoining one.

39.—*The Snail on the Flagstaff.*

It would often be interesting if we could trace back to their
origin many of the best known puzzles. Some of them would be
found to have been first propounded in very ancient times, and
there can be very little doubt that while a certain number may
have improved with age, others will have deteriorated and even

lost their original point and bearing. It is curious to find in the
Solvamhall records our familiar friend the climbing snail puzzle,
and it will be seen that in its modern form it has lost its original
subtlety.

On the occasion of some great rejoicings at the Castle, Sir Hugh was superintending the flying of flags and banners, when somebody pointed out that a wandering snail was climbing up the flagstaff. One wise old fellow said :—

"They do say, Sir Knight, albeit I hold such stories as mere fables, that the snail doth climb upwards three feet in the daytime, but slippeth back two feet by night."

"Then," replied Sir Hugh, "tell us how many days it will take this snail to get from the bottom to the top of the pole."

"By bread and water, I much marvel if the same can be done unless we take down and measure the staff."

"Credit me," replied the knight, "there is no need to measure the staff."

Can the reader give the answer to this version of a puzzle that we all know so well ?

40.—*Lady Isabel's Casket.*

Sir Hugh's young kinswoman and ward, Lady Isabel de Fitz-arnulph, was known far and wide as " Isabel the Fair." Amongst her treasures was a casket, the top of which was perfectly square in shape. It was inlaid with pieces of wood, and a strip of gold ten inches long by a quarter of an inch wide.

When young men sued for the hand of Lady Isabel, Sir Hugh promised his consent to the one who would tell him the dimensions of the top of the box from these facts alone : that there was a rectangular strip of gold, ten inches by $\frac{1}{4}$-inch ; and the rest of the surface was exactly inlaid with pieces of wood, each piece being a perfect square, and no two pieces of the same size. Many young men failed, but one at length succeeded. The puzzle is not an easy one, but the dimensions of that strip of gold, combined with those other conditions, absolutely determine the size of the top of the casket.

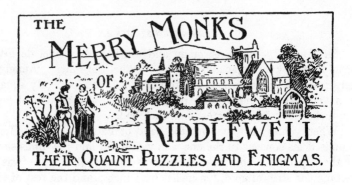

THE MERRY MONKS OF RIDDLEWELL

THEIR QUAINT PUZZLES AND ENIGMAS.

"FRIAR ANDREW," quoth the Lord Abbot, as he lay a-dying, "methinks I could now rede thee the riddle of riddles—an I had—the time—and—" The good friar put his ear close to the holy Abbot's lips, but alas! they were silenced for ever. Thus passed away the life of the jovial and greatly beloved Abbot of the old monastery of Riddlewell.

The monks of Riddlewell Abbey were noted in their day for the quaint enigmas and puzzles that they were in the habit of propounding. The Abbey was built in the fourteenth century, near a sacred spring known as the Red-hill Well. This became in the vernacular Reddlewell and Riddlewell, and under the Lord Abbot David the monks evidently tried to justify the latter form by the riddles they propounded so well. The solving of puzzles became the favourite recreation, no matter whether they happened to be of a metaphysical, philosophical, mathematical, or mechanical kind. It grew into an absorbing passion with them, and as I have shown above, in the case of the Abbot this passion was strong even in death.

It would seem that the words " puzzle," " problem," " enigma," etc., did not occur in their vocabulary. They were accustomed to call every poser a " riddle," no matter whether it took the form of " Where was Moses when the light went out ? " or the Squaring of the Circle. On one of the walls in the refectory were inscribed the words of Samson, " I will now put forth a riddle to you," to remind the brethren of what was expected of them, and the rule was that each monk in turn should propose some riddle weekly to the community, the others being always free to cap it with another if disposed to do so. Abbot David was, undoubtedly, the puzzle genius of the monastery, and everybody naturally bowed to his decision. Only a few of the Abbey riddles have been preserved, and I propose to select those that seem most interesting. I shall try to make the conditions of the puzzles perfectly clear, so that the modern reader may fully understand them, and be amused in trying to find some of the solutions.

41.—*The Riddle of the Fish-pond.*

At the bottom of the Abbey meads was a small fish-pond where the monks used to spend many a contemplative hour with rod and

line. One day, when they had had very bad luck and only caught twelve fishes amongst them, Brother Jonathan suddenly declared that as there was no sport that day he would put forth a riddle for their entertainment. He thereupon took twelve fish baskets and placed them at equal distances round the pond, as shown in our illustration, with one fish in each basket.

" Now, gentle anglers," said he, " rede me this riddle of the Twelve Fishes. Start at any basket you like, and, always going in one direction round the pond, take up one fish, pass it over two other fishes, and place it in the next basket. Go on again ; take up another single fish, and, having passed that also over two fishes, place it in a basket ; and so continue your journey. Six fishes only are to be removed, and when these have been placed, there should be two fishes in each of six baskets, and six baskets empty. Which of you merry wights will do this in such a manner that you shall go round the pond as few times as possible ? "

I will explain to the reader that it does not matter whether the two fishes that are passed over are in one or two baskets, nor how many empty baskets you pass. And, as Brother Jonathan said, you must always go in one direction round the pond (without any doubling back) and end at the spot from which you set out.

42.—*The Riddle of the Pilgrims.*

One day, when the monks were seated at their repast, the Abbot announced that a messenger had that morning brought news that a number of pilgrims were on the road and would require their hospitality.

" You will put them," he said, " in the square dormitory that has two floors with eight rooms on each floor. There must be eleven persons sleeping on each side of the building, and twice as many on the upper floor as on the lower floor. Of course every room must be occupied, and you know my rule that not more than three persons may occupy the same room."

I give a plan of the two floors, from which it will be seen that the sixteen rooms are approached by a well staircase in the centre. After the monks had solved this little problem and arranged for the accommodation, the pilgrims arrived, when it was found that they were three more in number than was at first stated. This necessitated a reconsideration of the question, but the wily monks

PLAN OF DORMITORY.

Eight Rooms on Upper Floor.   Eight Rooms on Lower Floor.

succeeded in getting over the new difficulty without breaking the Abbot's rules. The curious point of this puzzle is to discover the total number of pilgrims.

43.—*The Riddle of the Tiled Hearth.*

It seems that it was Friar Andrew who first managed to " rede the riddle of the Tiled Hearth." Yet it was a simple enough little puzzle. The square hearth, where they burnt their Yule logs and round which they had such merry carousings, was floored with sixteen large ornamental tiles. When these became cracked and burnt with the heat of the great fire, it was decided to put down new tiles, which had to be selected from four different patterns (the Cross, the Fleur-de-lys, the Lion, and the Star) ; but plain tiles were also available. The Abbot proposed that they should be laid as shown in our sketch, without any plain tiles at all ; but Brother Richard broke in,—

" I trow, my Lord Abbot, that a riddle is required of me this day. Listen, then, to that which I shall put forth. Let these sixteen tiles be so placed that no tile shall be in line with another of the same design "—(he meant, of course, not in line horizontally, vertically, or diagonally)—" and in such manner that as few plain

tiles as possible be required." When the monks handed in their plans it was found that only Friar Andrew had hit upon the correct answer, even Friar Richard himself being wrong. All had used too many plain tiles.

44.—*The Riddle of the Sack Wine.*

One evening, when seated at table, Brother Benjamin was called upon by the Abbot to give the riddle that was that day demanded of him.

"Forsooth," said he, " I am no good at the making of riddles, as thou knowest full well ; but I have been teasing my poor brain over a matter that I trust some among you will expound to me, for I cannot rede it myself. It is this. Mark me take a glass of sack from this bottle that contains a pint of wine and pour it into that jug which contains a pint of water. Now, I fill the glass with the mixture from the jug and pour it back into the bottle holding

the sack.   Pray tell me, have I taken more wine from the bottle
than water from the jug ?   Or have I taken more water from the
jug than wine from the bottle ? "

I gather that the monks got nearer to a great quarrel over this
little poser than had ever happened before.   One brother so far
forgot himself as to tell his neighbour that " more wine had got into
his pate than wit came out of it," while another noisily insisted that
it all depended on the shape of the glass and the age of the wine.
But the Lord Abbot intervened, showed them what a simple
question it really was, and restored good feeling all round.

45.—*The Riddle of the Cellarer.*

Then Abbot David looked grave, and said that this incident
brought to his mind the painful fact that John the Cellarer had

been caught robbing the cask of best Malvoisie that was reserved
for special occasions.   He ordered him to be brought in.

" Now, varlet," said the Abbot, as the ruddy-faced Cellarer

came before him, " thou knowest that thou wast taken this morning in the act of stealing good wine that was forbidden thee.   What hast thou to say for thyself ? "

" Prithee, my Lord Abbot, forgive me ! " he cried, falling on his knees.   " Of a truth, the Evil One did come and tempt me, and the cask was so handy, and the wine was so good withal, and —and I had drunk of it ofttimes without being found out, and—"

" Rascal ! that but maketh thy fault the worse ! How much wine hast thou taken ? "

" Alack-a-day !   There were a hundred pints in the cask at the start, and I have taken me a pint every day this month of June— it being to-day the thirtieth thereof—and if my Lord Abbot can tell me to a nicety how much good wine I have taken in all, let him punish me as he will."

" Why, knave, that is thirty pints."

" Nay, nay ; for each time I drew a pint out of the cask, I put in a pint of water in its stead ! "

It is a curious fact that this is the only riddle in the old record that is not accompanied by its solution.   Is it possible that it proved too hard a nut for the monks ?   There is merely the note, " John suffered no punishment for his sad fault."

46.—*The Riddle of the Crusaders.*

On another occasion a certain knight, Sir Ralph de Bohun, was a guest of the monks at Riddlewell Abbey.   Towards the close of a sumptuous repast he spoke as follows :—

" My Lord Abbot, knowing full well that riddles are greatly to thy liking, I will, by your leave, put forth one that was told unto me in foreign lands.   A body of Crusaders went forth to fight the good cause, and such was their number that they were able to form themselves into a square.   But on the way a stranger took up arms and joined them, and they were then able to form exactly thirteen smaller squares.   Pray tell me, merry monks, how many men went forth to battle ? "

Abbot David pushed aside his plate of warden pie, and made a few hasty calculations.

"Sir Knight," said he at length, "the riddle is easy to rede. In the first place there were 324 men, who would make a square 18 by 18, and afterwards 325 men would make 13 squares of 25

Crusaders each. But which of you can tell me how many men there would have been if, instead of 13, they had been able to form 113 squares under exactly the like conditions ? "

The monks gave up this riddle, but the Abbot showed them the answer next morning.

47.—The Riddle of St. Edmondsbury.

" It used to be told at St. Edmondsbury," said Father Peter on one occasion, " that many years ago they were so overrun with mice that the good abbot gave orders that all the cats from the country round should be obtained to exterminate the vermin. A record was kept, and at the end of the year it was found that every cat had killed an equal number of mice, and the total was exactly 1,111,111 mice. How many cats do you suppose there were ? "

" Methinks one cat killed the lot," said Brother Benjamin.

" Out upon thee, brother ! I said ' cats.' "

" Well, then," persisted Benjamin, " perchance 1,111,111 cats each killed one mouse."

" No," replied Father Peter, after the monks' jovial laughter had ended, " I said ' mice ; ' and all I need add is this—that each cat killed more mice than there were cats. They told me it was merely a question of the division of numbers, but I know not the answer to the riddle."

The correct answer is recorded, but it is not shown how they arrived at it.

48.—*The Riddle of the Frogs' Ring.*

One Christmas the Abbot offered a prize of a large black jack mounted in silver, to be engraved with the name of the monk who should put forth the best new riddle. This tournament of wit was won by Brother Benedict, who, curiously enough, never before or after gave out anything that did not excite the ridicule of his brethren. It was called the " Frogs' Ring."

A ring was made with chalk on the floor of the hall, and divided into thirteen compartments, in which twelve discs of wood (called " frogs ") were placed in the order shown in our illustration, one place being left vacant. The numbers 1 to 6 were painted white and the numbers 7 to 12 black. The puzzle was to get all the white numbers where the black ones were, and *vice versa*. The white frogs move round in one direction, and the black ones the opposite way. They may move in any order one step at a time, or jumping over one of the opposite colour to the place beyond, just as we play draughts to-day. The only other condition is that when all the frogs have changed sides, the 1 must be where the 12 now is and the 12 in the place now occupied by 1. The puzzle was to perform the feat in as few moves as possible. How many moves are necessary ?

I will conclude in the words of the old writer : " These be some of the riddles which the monks of Riddlewell did set forth and expound each to the others in the merry days of the good Abbot David."

THE STRANGE ESCAPE OF THE KING'S JESTER.

A PUZZLING ADVENTURE.

At one time I was greatly in favour with the king, and his Majesty never seemed to weary of the companionship of the court fool. I had a gift for making riddles and quaint puzzles which ofttimes caused great sport; for albeit the king never found the right answer of one of these things in all his life, yet would he make merry at the bewilderment of those about him.

But let every cobbler stick unto his last; for when I did set out to learn the art of performing strange tricks in the magic, wherein the hand doth ever deceive the eye, the king was affrighted, and did accuse me of being a wizard, even commanding that I should be put to death. Luckily my wit did save my life. I begged that I might be slain by the royal hand and not by that of the executioner.

"By the saints," said his Majesty, "what difference can it make unto thee? But since it is thy wish, thou shalt have thy choice whether I kill thee or the executioner."

"Your Majesty," I answered, "I accept the choice that thou hast so graciously offered to me: I prefer that your Majesty should kill the executioner."

Yet is the life of a royal jester beset with great dangers, and the king having once gotten it into his royal head that I was a wizard, it was not long before I again fell into trouble, from which my wit did not a second time in a like way save me. I was cast into the dungeon to await my death. How, by the help of my gift in answering riddles and puzzles, I did escape from captivity I will now set forth; and in case it doth perplex any to know how some of the strange feats were performed, I will hereafter make the manner thereof plain to all.

49.—*The Mysterious Rope.*

My dungeon did not lie beneath the moat, but was in one of the most high parts of the castle. So stout was the door, and so well

locked and secured withal, that escape that way was not to be found. By hard work I did, after many days, remove one of the bars from the narrow window, and was able to crush my body through the opening; but the distance to the courtyard below was so exceeding great that it was certain death to drop thereto. Yet by great good fortune did I find in the corner of the cell a rope that had been there left and lay hid in the great darkness. But this rope had not length enough, and to drop in safety from the end was nowise possible. Then did I remember how the wise man from Ireland did lengthen the blanket that was too short for him by cutting a yard off the bottom of the same and joining it on to the top. So I made haste to divide the rope in half and to tie the two parts thereof together again. It was then full long, and did reach the ground, and I went down in safety. How could this have been?

50.—*The Underground Maze.*

The only way out of the yard that I now was in was to descend a few stairs that led up into the centre (A) of an underground maze, through the winding of which I must pass before I could take my leave by the door (B). But I knew full well that in the great darkness of this dreadful place I might well wander for hours and yet return to the place from which I set out. How was I then

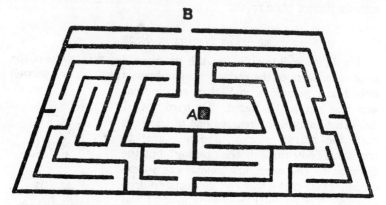

to reach the door with certainty? With a plan of the maze it is but a simple matter to trace out the route, but how was the way to be found in the place itself in utter darkness?

51.—*The Secret Lock.*

When I did at last reach the door it was fast closed, and on sliding a panel set before a grating the light that came in thereby showed unto me that my passage was barred by the king's secret lock. Before the handle of the door might be turned, it was needful to place the hands of three several dials in their proper places. If you but knew the proper letter for each dial, the secret was of a truth to your hand; but as ten letters were upon the face of every dial, you might try nine hundred and ninety-nine times and only succeed on the thousandth attempt withal. If I was indeed to escape I must waste not a moment.

Now, once had I heard the learned monk who did invent the lock say that he feared that the king's servants, having such bad memories, would mayhap forget the right letters; so perchance, thought I, he had on this account devised some way to aid their memories. And what more natural than to make the letters

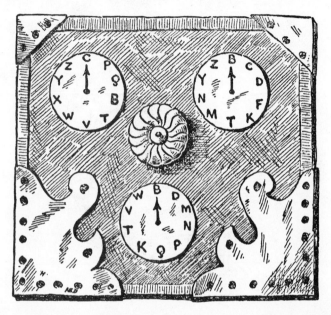

form some word? I soon found a word that was English, made of three letters—one letter being on each of the three dials. After that I had pointed the hands properly to the letters the door opened and I passed out. What was the secret word?

52.—*Crossing the Moat.*

I was now face to face with the castle moat, which was, indeed, very wide and very deep. Alas! I could not swim, and my chance of escape seemed of a truth hopeless, as, doubtless, it would have been had I not espied a boat tied to the wall by a rope. But after I had got into it I did find that the oars had been taken away, and that there was nothing that I could use to row me across.   When I had untied the rope and pushed off upon the water the boat lay

quite still, there being no stream or current to help me.   How, then, did I yet take the boat across the moat ?

53.—*The Royal Gardens.*

It was now daylight, and still had I to pass through the royal gardens outside of the castle walls.   These gardens had once been laid out by an old king's gardener, who had become bereft of his senses, but was allowed to amuse himself therein.   They were square, and divided into 16 parts by high walls, as shown in the plan thereof, so that there were openings from one garden to an-

other, but only two different ways of entrance. Now, it was needful that I enter at the gate A and leave by the other gate B ; but
as there were gardeners going and coming about their work, I had
to slip with agility from one garden to another, so that I might not

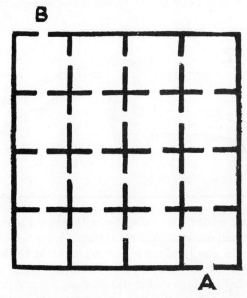

be seen, but escape unobserved. I did succeed in so doing, but
afterwards remembered that I had of a truth entered every one
of the 16 gardens once, and never more than once. This was,
indeed, a curious thing. How might it have been done ?

54.—*Bridging the Ditch.*

I now did truly think that at last was I a free man, but I had
quite forgot that I must yet cross a deep ditch before I might get
right away. This ditch was 10 feet wide, and I durst not attempt
to jump it, as I had sprained an ankle in leaving the garden. Looking around for something to help me over my difficulty, I soon

found eight narrow planks of wood lying together in a heap. With these alone, and the planks were each no more than 9 feet long, I did at last manage to make a bridge across the ditch. How was this done ?

Being now free I did hasten to the house of a friend who pro-

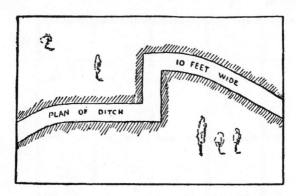

vided me with a horse and a disguise, with which I soon succeeded in placing myself out of all fear of capture.

Through the goodly offices of divers persons at the king's court I did at length obtain the royal pardon, though, indeed, I was never restored to that full favour that was once my joy and pride.

Ofttimes have I been asked by many that do know me to set forth to them the strange manner of my escape, which more than one hath deemed to be of a truth wonderful, albeit the feat was nothing astonishing withal if we do but remember that from my youth upwards I had trained my wit to the making and answering of cunning enigmas. And I do hold that the study of such crafty matters is good, not alone for the pleasure that is created thereby, but because a man may never be sure that in some sudden and untoward difficulty that may beset him in passing through this life of ours such strange learning may not serve his ends greatly, and, mayhap, help him out of many difficulties.

I am now an aged man, and have not quite lost all my taste

for quaint puzzles and conceits; but, of a truth, never have I found greater pleasure in making out the answers to any of these things than I had in mastering them that did enable me, as the king's jester in disgrace, to gain my freedom from the castle dungeon and so save my life.

THE SQUIRE'S CHRISTMAS PUZZLE PARTY

A FINE specimen of the old English country gentleman was Squire Davidge, of Stoke Courcy Hall, in Somerset. When the last century was yet in its youth, there were few men in the west country more widely known and more generally respected and beloved than he. A born sportsman, his fame extended to Exmoor itself, where his daring and splendid riding in pursuit of the red deer had excited the admiration and envy of innumerable younger huntsmen. But it was in his own parish, and particularly in his own home, that his genial hospitality, generosity, and rare jovial humour made him the idol of his friends—and even of his relations, which sometimes means a good deal.

At Christmas it was always an open house at Stoke Courcy Hall, for if there was one thing more than another upon which Squire Davidge had very pronounced views, it was on the question of keeping up in a royal fashion the great festival of Yule-tide. "Hark ye, my lads," he would say to his sons: "our country will begin to fall on evil days if ever we grow indifferent to the claims of those Christmas festivities that have helped to win us the proud name of Merrie England." Therefore, when I say that Christmas at Stoke Courcy was kept up in the good old happy, rollicking, festive style that our grandfathers and great-grandfathers so dearly loved, it will be unnecessary for me to attempt a description. We have a faithful picture of these merry scenes in the *Bracebridge Hall* of Washington Irving. I must confine myself in this sketch to one special feature in the Squire's round of jollification during the season of peace and good will.

He took a curious and intelligent interest in puzzles of every kind, and there was always one night devoted to what was known as " Squire Davidge's Puzzle Party." Every guest was expected to come armed with some riddle or puzzle for the bewilderment and possible delectation of the company. The old gentleman always presented a new watch to the guest who was most successful in his answers. It is a pity that all the puzzles were not preserved; but I propose to present to my readers a few selected from a number that have passed down to a surviving member of the family, who has kindly allowed me to use them on this occasion. There are some very easy ones, a few that are moderately difficult, and one hard brain-racker, so all should be able to find something to their taste.

The little record is written in the neat angular hand of a young lady of that day, and the puzzles, the conditions of which I think it best to give mainly in my own words for the sake of greater clearness, appear to have been all propounded on one occasion.

55.—*The Three Teacups.*

One young lady—of whom our fair historian records with delightful inconsequence : " This Miss Charity Lockyer has since been married to a curate from Taunton Vale "—placed three empty

teacups on a table, and challenged anybody to put ten lumps of sugar in them so that there would be an odd number of lumps in every cup. " One young man, who has been to Oxford University, and is studying the law, declared with some heat that, beyond a doubt, there was no possible way of doing it, and he offered to give proof of the fact to the company." It must have been interesting to see his face when he was shown Miss Charity's correct answer.

56.—*The Eleven Pennies.*

A guest asked some one to favour him with eleven pennies, and he passed the coins to the company, as depicted in our illustration. The writer says : " He then requested us to remove five coins from

the eleven, add four coins and leave nine.   We could not but think there must needs be ten pennies left.   We were a good deal amused at the answer hereof."

57.—*The Christmas Geese.*

Squire Hembrow, from Weston Zoyland—wherever that may be—proposed the following little arithmetical puzzle, from which it is probable that several somewhat similar modern ones have been derived : Farmer Rouse sent his man to market with a flock of geese, telling him that he might sell all or any of them, as he considered best, for he was sure the man knew how to make a good bargain.   This is the report that Jabez made, though I have taken it out of the old Somerset dialect, which might puzzle some readers in a way not desired. "Well, first of all I sold Mr. Jasper Tyler half of the flock and half a goose over; then I sold Farmer Avent a third of what remained and a third of a goose over; then I sold Widow Foster a quarter of what remained and three-quarters of a goose over; and as I was coming home, whom should I meet but Ned Collier: so we had a mug of cider together at the Barley Mow, where I sold him exactly a fifth of what I had left, and gave him a fifth of a goose over for the missus. These nineteen that I have brought back I couldn't get rid of at any price." Now, how many geese did Farmer Rouse send to market? My humane readers may be relieved to know that no goose was divided or put to any inconvenience whatever by the sales.

58.—*The Chalked Numbers.*

"We laughed greatly at a pretty jest on the part of Major Trenchard, a merry friend of the Squire's. With a piece of chalk he marked a different number on the backs of eight lads who were at the party." Then, it seems, he divided them in two groups, as shown in the illustration, 1, 2, 3, 4 being on one side, and 5, 7, 8, 9 on the other. It will be seen that the numbers of the left-hand group add up to 10, while the numbers in the other group add up to 29. The Major's puzzle was to rearrange the eight boys in two new groups, so that the four numbers in each group should add up alike. The Squire's niece asked if the 5 should not be a 6; but the Major explained that the numbers were quite correct if properly regarded.

59.—*Tasting the Plum Puddings.*

" Everybody, as I suppose, knows well that the number of different Christmas plum puddings that you taste will bring you the same number of lucky days in the new year. One of the guests (and his name has escaped my memory) brought with him a sheet of paper on which were drawn sixty-four puddings, and he said the puzzle was an allegory of a sort, and he intended to show how we might manage our pudding-tasting with as much dispatch as possible." I fail to fully understand this fanciful and rather overstrained view of the puzzle. But it would appear that the puddings were arranged regularly, as I have shown them in the illustration, and that to strike out a pudding was to indicate that it had been duly tasted. You have simply to put the point of your pencil on the pudding in the top corner, bearing a sprig of holly, and strike out all the sixty-four puddings through their centres in twenty-one straight strokes. You can go up or down or horizontally, but not diagonally or obliquely; and you must never strike out a pudding twice, as that would imply a second and unnecessary tasting of those indigestible dainties. But the peculiar part of the thing is that you are required to taste the pudding that is seen steaming hot at the end of your tenth stroke, and to taste the one decked with holly in the bottom row the very last of all.

60.—*Under the Mistletoe Bough.*

" At the party was a widower who has but lately come into these parts," says the record; "and, to be sure, he was an exceedingly melancholy man, for he did sit away from the company during the most part of the evening. We afterwards heard that he had been keeping a secret account of all the kisses that were given and received under the mistletoe bough, Truly, I would not have suffered any one to kiss me in that manner had I known that so unfair a watch was being kept. Other maids beside were in a like way shocked, as Betty Marchant has since told me." But it seems that the melancholy widower was merely collecting material for the following little osculatory problem.

The company consisted of the Squire and his wife and six other married couples, one widower and three widows, twelve bachelors and boys, and ten maidens and little girls. Now, everybody was found to have kissed everybody else, with the following exceptions and additions : No male, of course, kissed a male. No married man kissed a married woman, except his own wife. All the bachelors and boys kissed all the maidens and girls twice. The widower did not kiss anybody, and the widows did not kiss each other. The puzzle was to ascertain just how many kisses had been

thus given under the mistletoe bough, assuming, as it is charitable to do, that every kiss was returned—the double act being counted as one kiss.

61.—*The Silver Cubes.*

The last extract that I will give is one that will, I think, interest those readers who may find some of the above puzzles too easy.

It is a hard nut, and should only be attempted by those who flatter themselves that they possess strong intellectual teeth.

"Master Herbert Spearing, the son of a widow lady in our parish, proposed a puzzle in arithmetic that looks simple, but nobody present was able to solve it. Of a truth I did not venture to attempt it myself, after the young lawyer from Oxford, who they say is very learned in the mathematics and a great scholar, failed to show us the answer. He did assure us that he believed it could not be done, but I have since been told that it is possible, though, of a certainty, I may not vouch for it. Master Herbert brought with him two cubes of solid silver that belonged to his

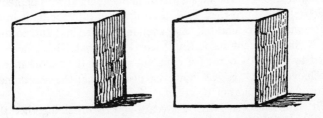

mother. He showed that, as they measured two inches every way, each contained eight cubic inches of silver, and therefore the two contained together sixteen cubic inches. That which he wanted to know was—' Could anybody give him exact dimensions for two cubes that should together contain just seventeen cubic inches of silver?'" Of course the cubes may be of different sizes.

The idea of a Christmas Puzzle Party, as devised by the old Squire, seems to have been excellent, and it might well be revived at the present day by people who are fond of puzzles and who have grown tired of Book Teas and similar recent introductions for the amusement of evening parties. Prizes could be awarded to the best solvers of the puzzles propounded by the guests.

ADVENTURES OF · THE · PUZZLE·CLUB·

WHEN it recently became known that the bewildering mystery of the Prince and the Lost Balloon was really solved by the members of the Puzzle Club, the general public was quite unaware that any such club existed. The fact is that the members always deprecated publicity ; but since they have been dragged into the light in connection with this celebrated case, so many absurd and untrue stories have become current respecting their doings that I have been permitted to publish a correct account of some of their more interesting achievements. It was, however, decided that the real names of the members should not be given.

The club was started a few years ago to bring together those interested in the solution of puzzles of all kinds, and it contains some of the profoundest mathematicians and some of the most subtle thinkers resident in London. These have done some excellent work of a high and dry kind. But the main body soon took to investigating the problems of real life that are perpetually cropping up.

It is only right to say that they take no interest in crimes as such, but only investigate a case when it possesses features of a distinctly puzzling character. They seek perplexity for its own sake—something to unravel. As often as not the circumstances are of no importance to anybody, but they just form a little puzzle in real life, and that is sufficient.

62.—The Ambiguous Photograph.

A good example of the lighter kind of problem that occasionally comes before them is that which is known amongst them by the name of " The Ambiguous Photograph." Though it is perplexing to the inexperienced, it is regarded in the club as quite a trivial thing. Yet it serves to show the close observation of these sharp-witted fellows. The original photograph hangs on the club wall, and has baffled every guest who has examined it. Yet any child should be able to solve the mystery. I will give the reader an opportunity of trying his wits at it.

Some of the members were one evening seated together in their clubhouse in the Adelphi. Those present were : Henry Melville, a barrister not overburdened with briefs, who was discussing a problem with Ernest Russell, a bearded man of middle age, who held some easy post in Somerset House, and was a Senior Wrangler and one of the most subtle thinkers of the club ; Fred Wilson, a journalist of very buoyant spirits, who had more real capacity than one would at first suspect ; John Macdonald, a Scotsman, whose record was that he had never solved a puzzle himself since the club was formed, though frequently he had put others on the track of a deep solution ; Tim Churton, a bank clerk, full of cranky, unorthodox ideas as to perpetual motion ; also Harold Tomkins, a prosperous accountant, remarkably familiar with the elegant branch of matnematics—the theory of numbers.

Suddenly Herbert Baynes entered the room, and everybody saw at once from his face that he had something interesting to communicate. Baynes was a man of private means, with no occupation.

" Here's a quaint little poser for you all," said Baynes. " I have received it to-day from Dovey."

Dovey was proprietor of one of the many private detective agencies that found it to their advantage to keep in touch with the club.

" Is it another of those easy cryptograms ? " asked Wilson. " If so, I would suggest sending it upstairs to the billiard-marker."

" Don't be sarcastic, Wilson," said Melville. " Remember, we are indebted to Dovey for the great Railway Signal Problem that gave us all a week's amusement in the solving."

" If you fellows want to hear," resumed Baynes, " just try to keep quiet while I relate the amusing affair to you. You all know of the jealous little Yankee who married Lord Marksford two years ago ? Lady Marksford and her husband have been in Paris for two or three months. Well, the poor creature soon got under the influence of the green-eyed monster, and formed the opinion that Lord Marksford was flirting with other ladies of his acquaintance.

" Now, she has actually put one of Dovey's spies on to that excellent husband of hers ; and the myrmidon has been shadowing him about for a fortnight with a pocket camera. A few days ago he came to Lady Marksford in great glee. He had snapshotted his lordship while actually walking in the public streets with a lady who was not his wife."

" ' What is the use of this at all ? ' asked the jealous woman.

" ' Well, it is evidence, your ladyship, that your husband was walking with the lady. I know where she is staying, and in a few days shall have found out all about her.'

" ' But, you stupid man,' cried her ladyship, in tones of great contempt, ' how can any one swear that this is his lordship, when the greater part of him, including his head and shoulders, is hidden from sight ? And—and '—she scrutinized the photo carefully— ' why, I guess it is impossible from this photograph to say whether the gentleman is walking with the lady or going in the opposite direction ! '

" Thereupon she dismissed the detective in high dudgeon. Dovey has himself just returned from Paris, and got this account of the incident from her ladyship. He wants to justify his man, if possible, by showing that the photo does disclose which way the man is going. Here it is. See what you fellows can make of it."

Our illustration is a faithful drawing made from the original photograph. It will be seen that a slight but sudden summer shower is the real cause of the difficulty.

All agreed that Lady Marksford was right—that it is impossible to determine whether the man is walking with the lady or not.

"Her ladyship is wrong," said Baynes, after everybody had made a close scrutiny. "I find there is important evidence in the picture. Look at it carefully."

"Of course," said Melville, "we can tell nothing from the frock-coat. It may be the front or the tails. Blessed if I can say!"

Then he has his overcoat over his arm, but which way his arm goes it is impossible to see."

" How about the bend of the legs ? " asked Churton

" Bend ! why, there isn't any bend," put in Wilson, as he glanced over the other's shoulder. " From the picture you might suspect that his lordship has no knees. The fellow took his snapshot just when the legs happened to be perfectly straight."

" I'm thinking that perhaps——" began Macdonald, adjusting his eye-glasses.

" Don't think, Mac," advised Wilson. " It might hurt you. Besides, it is no use you thinking that if the dog would kindly pass on things would be easy. He won't."

" The man's general pose seems to me to imply movement to the left," Tomkins thought.

" On the contrary," Melville declared, " it appears to me clearly to suggest movement to the right."

" Now, look here, you men," said Russell, whose opinions

always carried respect in the club. " It strikes me that what we have to do is to consider the attitude of the lady rather than that of the man. Does her attention seem to be directed to somebody by her side ? "

Everybody agreed that it was impossible to say.

" I've got it ! " shouted Wilson. " Extraordinary that none of you have seen it. It is as clear as possible. It all came to me in a flash ! "

" Well, what is it ? " asked Baynes.

" Why, it is perfectly obvious. You see which way the dog is going—to the left. Very well. Now, Baynes, to whom does the dog belong ? "

" To the detective ! "

The laughter against Wilson that followed this announcement was simply boisterous, and so prolonged that Russell, who had at the time possession of the photo, seized the opportunity for making a most minute examination of it. In a few moments he held up his hands to invoke silence.

" Baynes is right," he said. " There is important evidence there which settles the matter with certainty. Assuming that the gentleman is really Lord Marksford—and the figure, so far as it is visible, is his—I have no hesitation myself in saying that——"

" Stop ! " all the members shouted at once.

" Don't break the rules of the club, Russell, though Wilson did," said Melville. " Recollect that ' no member shall openly disclose his solution to a puzzle unless all present consent.' "

" You need not have been alarmed," explained Russell. " I was simply going to say that I have no hesitation in declaring that Lord Marksford is walking in one particular direction. In which direction I will tell you when you have all ' given it up.' "

63.—*The Cornish Cliff Mystery.*

Though the incident known in the Club as " The Cornish Cliff Mystery " has never been published, every one remembers the case with which it was connected—an embezzlement at Todd's Bank in Cornhill a few years ago. Lamson and Marsh, two of the firm's clerks, suddenly disappeared ; and it was found that they had absconded with a very large sum of money. There was an exciting hunt for them by the police, who were so prompt in their action that it was impossible for the thieves to get out of the country. They were traced as far as Truro, and were known to be in hiding in Cornwall.

Just at this time it happened that Henry Melville and Fred Wilson were away together on a walking tour round the Cornish coast. Like most people, they were interested in the case ; and one morning, while at breakfast at a little inn, they learnt that the absconding men had been tracked to that very neighbourhood, and that a strong cordon of police had been drawn round the district, making an escape very improbable. In fact, an inspector and a constable came into the inn to make some inquiries, and exchanged civilities with the two members of the Puzzle Club. A few references to some of the leading London detectives, and the production of a confidential letter Melville happened to have in his pocket from one of them, soon established complete confidence, and the inspector opened out.

He said that he had just been to examine a very important clue a quarter of a mile from there, and expressed the opinion that Messrs. Lamson and Marsh would never again be found alive. At the suggestion of Melville the four men walked along the road together.

" There is our stile in the distance," said the inspector. " This constable found beside it the pocket-book that I have shown you, containing the name of Marsh and some memoranda in his handwriting. It had evidently been dropped by accident. On looking over the stone stile he noticed the footprints of two men—which I have already proved from particulars previously supplied to the police to be those of the men we want—and I am sure you will agree that they point to only one possible conclusion."

Arrived at the spot, they left the hard road and got over the stile. The footprints of the two men were here very clearly impressed in the thin but soft soil, and they all took care not to trample on the tracks. They followed the prints closely, and found that they led straight to the edge of a cliff forming a sheer precipice, almost perpendicular, at the foot of which the sea, some two hundred feet below, was breaking among the boulders.

" Here, gentlemen, you see," said the inspector, " that the footprints lead straight to the edge of the cliff, where there is a good

deal of trampling about, and there end. The soil has nowhere been disturbed for yards around, except by the footprints that you see. The conclusion is obvious."

" That, knowing they were unable to escape capture, they decided not to be taken alive, and threw themselves over the cliff ? " asked Wilson.

" Exactly. Look to the right and the left, and you will find no footprints or other marks anywhere. Go round there to the left, and you will be satisfied that the most experienced mountaineer that ever lived could not make a descent, or even anywhere get over the edge of the cliff. There is no ledge or foothold within fifty feet."

"Utterly impossible," said Melville, after an inspection. "What do you propose to do ? "

"I am going straight back to communicate the discovery to headquarters. We shall withdraw the cordon and search the coast for the dead bodies."

"Then you will make a fatal mistake," said Melville. "The men are alive and in hiding in the district. Just examine the prints again. Whose is the large foot ? "

"That is Lamson's, and the small print is Marsh's. Lamson was a tall man, just over six feet, and Marsh was a little fellow."

"I thought as much," said Melville. "And yet you will find that Lamson takes a shorter stride than Marsh. Notice, also, the peculiarity that Marsh walks heavily on his heels, while Lamson treads more on his toes. Nothing remarkable in that ? Perhaps not ; but has it occurred to you that Lamson walked behind Marsh ? Because you will find that he sometimes treads over Marsh's foot-steps, though you will never find Marsh treading in the steps of the other."

"Do you suppose that the men walked backwards in their own footprints ? " asked the inspector.

"No ; that is impossible. No two men could walk backwards some two hundred yards in that way with such exactitude. You will not find a single place where they have missed the print by even an eighth of an inch. Quite impossible. Nor do I suppose that two men, hunted as they were, could have provided themselves with flying-machines, balloons, or even parachutes. They did not drop over the cliff."

Melville then explained how the men had got away. His account proved to be quite correct, for it will be remembered that they were caught, hiding under some straw in a barn, within two miles of the spot. How did they get away from the edge of the cliff ?

64.—*The Runaway Motor-Car.*

The little affair of the " Runaway Motor-car " is a good illustration of how a knowledge of some branch of puzzledom may be put
to unexpected use.   A member of the Club, whose name I have
at the moment of writing forgotten, came in one night and said
that a friend of his was bicycling in Surrey on the previous day,
when a motor-car came from behind, round a corner, at a terrific
speed, caught one of his wheels, and sent him flying in the road.
He was badly knocked about, and fractured his left arm, while
his machine was wrecked.   The motor-car was not stopped, and
he had been unable to trace it.

There were two witnesses to the accident, which was beyond
question the fault of the driver of the car.   An old woman, a Mrs.
Wadey, saw the whole thing, and tried to take the number of the
car.   She was positive as to the letters, which need not be given,
and was certain also that the first figure was a 1.   The other figures
she failed to read on account of the speed and dust.

The other witness was the village simpleton, who just escapes
being an arithmetical genius, but is excessively stupid in everything else.

He is always working out sums in his head ; and all he could say
was that there were five figures in the number, and that he found
that when he multiplied the first two figures by the last three they
made the same figures, only in different order—just as 24 multiplied
by 651 makes 15,624 (the same five figures), in which case the
number of the car would have been 24,651 ; and he knew there
was no 0 in the number.

" It will be easy enough to find that car," said Russell.   " The
known facts are possibly sufficient to enable one to discover the
exact number.   You see, there must be a limit to the five-figure
numbers having the peculiarity observed by the simpleton.   And
these are further limited by the fact that, as Mrs. Wadey states,
the number began with the figure 1.   We have therefore to find
these numbers.   It may conceivably happen that there is only

one such number, in which case the thing is solved. But even if there are several cases, the owner of the actual car may easily be found.

" How will you manage that ? " somebody asked.

" Surely," replied Russell, " the method is quite obvious. By

the process of elimination. Every owner except the one in fault will be able to prove an alibi. Yet, merely guessing offhand, I think it quite probable that there is only one number that fits the case. We shall see."

Russell was right, for that very night he sent the number by post, with the result that the runaway car was at once traced, and its owner, who was himself driving, had to pay the cost of the damages resulting from his carelessness. What was the number of the car ?

65.—*The Mystery of Ravensdene Park.*

The mystery of Ravensdene Park, which I will now present, was a tragic affair, as it involved the assassination of Mr. Cyril Hastings at his country house a short distance from London.

On February 17th, at 11 p.m., there was a heavy fall of snow, and though it lasted only half an hour, the ground was covered to a depth of several inches. Mr. Hastings had been spending the evening at the house of a neighbour, and left at midnight to walk home, taking the short route that lay through Ravensdene Park—

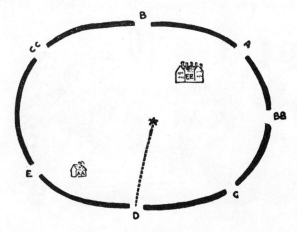

that is, from D to A in the sketch-plan.   But in the early morning he was found dead, at the point indicated by the star in our diagram, stabbed to the heart.   All the seven gates were promptly closed, and the footprints in the snow examined.   These were fortunately very distinct, and the police obtained the following facts :—

The footprints of Mr. Hastings were very clear, straight from D to the spot where he was found.   There were the footprints of the Ravensdene butler—who retired to bed five minutes before midnight—from E to EE.   There were the footprints of the game-keeper from A to his lodge at AA.   Other footprints showed that one individual had come in at gate B and left at gate BB, while another had entered by gate C and left at gate CC.

Only these five persons had entered the park since the fall of snow. Now, it was a very foggy night, and some of these pedestrians had consequently taken circuitous routes, but it was particularly noticed that no track ever crossed another track. Of this the police were absolutely certain, but they stupidly omitted to make a sketch of the various routes before the snow had melted and utterly effaced them.

The mystery was brought before the members of the Puzzle Club, who at once set themselves the task of solving it. Was it

possible to discover who committed the crime? Was it the butler? Or the gamekeeper? Or the man who came in at B and went out at BB? Or the man who went in at C and left at CC? They provided themselves with diagrams—sketch-plans, like the one we have reproduced, which simplified the real form of Ravensdene Park without destroying the necessary conditions of the problem.

Our friends then proceeded to trace out the route of each person, in accordance with the positive statements of the police that we have given. It was soon evident that, as no path ever crossed another, some of the pedestrians must have lost their way considerably in the fog. But when the tracks were recorded in all possible ways, they had no difficulty in deciding on the assassin's route ; and as the police luckily knew whose footprints this route represented, an arrest was made that led to the man's conviction.

Can our readers discover whether A, B, C, or E committed the deed ? Just trace out the route of each of the four persons, and the key to the mystery will reveal itself.

66.—*The Buried Treasure.*

The problem of the Buried Treasure was of quite a different character. A young fellow named Dawkins, just home from Australia, was introduced to the club by one of the members, in order that he might relate an extraordinary stroke of luck that he had experienced " down under," as the circumstances involved the solution of a poser that could not fail to interest all lovers of puzzle problems. After the club dinner, Dawkins was asked to tell his story, which he did, to the following effect :—

" I have told you, gentlemen, that I was very much down on my luck. I had gone out to Australia to try to retrieve my fortunes, but had met with no success, and the future was looking very dark. I was, in fact, beginning to feel desperate. One hot summer day I happened to be seated in a Melbourne wineshop, when two fellows entered, and engaged in conversation. They thought I was asleep, but I assure you I was very wide awake.

" ' If only I could find the right field,' said one man, ' the treasure would be mine ; and as the original owner left no heir, I have as much right to it as anybody else.'

" ' How would you proceed ? ' asked the other.

" ' Well, it is like this : The document that fell into my hands states clearly that the field is square, and that the treasure is buried in it at a point exactly two furlongs from one corner, three furlongs from the next corner, and four furlongs from the next corner to that. You see, the worst of it is that nearly all the fields in the district are square ; and I doubt whether there are two of exactly the same size.   If only I knew the size of the field I could soon discover it, and, by taking these simple measurements, quickly secure the treasure.'

" ' But you would not know which corner to start from, nor which direction to go to the next corner.'

" ' My dear chap, that only means eight spots at the most to

dig over ; and as the paper says that the treasure is three feet deep, you bet that wouldn't take me long.'

" Now, gentlemen," continued Dawkins, " I happen to be a bit of a mathematician ; and hearing the conversation, I saw at once that for a spot to be exactly two, three, and four furlongs from successive corners of a square, the square must be of a particular area.   You can't get such measurements to meet at one point in any square you choose.   They can only happen in a field of one size, and that is just what these men never suspected. I will leave you the puzzle of working out just what that area is.

"Well, when I found the size of the field, I was not long in discovering the field itself, for the man had let out the district in the conversation. And I did not need to make the eight digs, for, as luck would have it, the third spot I tried was the right one. The treasure was a substantial sum, for it has brought me home and enabled me to start in a business that already shows signs of being a particularly lucrative one. I often smile when I think of that poor fellow going about for the rest of his life saying : ' If only I knew the size of the field ! ' while he has placed the treasure safe in my own possession. I tried to find the man, to make him some compensation anonymously, but without success. Perhaps he stood in little need of the money, while it has saved me from ruin."

Could the reader have discovered the required area of the field from those details overheard in the wineshop ? It is an elegant little puzzle, and furnishes another example of the practical utility, on unexpected occasions, of a knowledge of the art of problem-solving.

THE PROFESSOR'S PUZZLES

" WHY, here is the Professor!" exclaimed Grigsby. "We'll make him show us some new puzzles."

It was Christmas Eve, and the club was nearly deserted. Only Grigsby, Hawkhurst, and myself, of all the members, seemed to be detained in town over the season of mirth and mincepies. The man, however, who had just entered was a welcome addition to our number. " The Professor of Puzzles," as we had nicknamed him, was very popular at the club, and when, as on the present occasion, things got a little slow, his arrival was a positive blessing.

He was a man of middle age, cheery and kind-hearted, but inclined to be cynical. He had all his life dabbled in puzzles, problems, and enigmas of every kind, and what the Professor didn't know about these matters was admittedly not worth knowing. His puzzles always had a charm of their own, and this was mainly because he was so happy in dishing them up in palatable form.

" You are the man of all others that we were hoping would drop in," said Hawkhurst. " Have you got anything new ? "

" I have always something new," was the reply, uttered with feigned conceit—for the Professor was really a modest man—" I'm simply glutted with ideas."

" Where do you get all your notions ? " I asked.

" Everywhere, anywhere, during all my waking moments. Indeed, two or three of my best puzzles have come to me in my dreams."

" Then all the good ideas are not used up ? "

" Certainly not. And all the old puzzles are capable of improvement, embellishment, and extension. Take, for example, magic squares. These were constructed in India before the Christian era, and introduced into Europe about the fourteenth century, when they were supposed to possess certain magical properties that I am afraid they have since lost. Any child can arrange the numbers one to nine in a square that will add up fifteen in eight ways ; but you will see it can be developed into quite a new problem if you use coins instead of numbers."

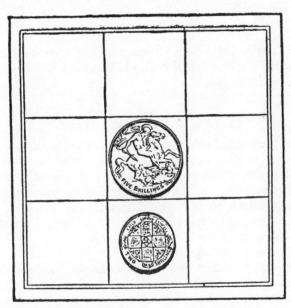

67.—*The Coinage Puzzle.*

He made a rough diagram, and placed a crown and a florin in two of the divisions, as indicated in the illustration.

" Now," he continued, " place the fewest possible current English coins in the seven empty divisions, so that each of the three columns, three rows, and two diagonals shall add up fifteen shillings. Of course, no division may be without at least one coin, and no two divisions may contain the same value."

" But how can the coins affect the question ? " asked Grigsby.

" That you will find out when you approach the solution."

" I shall do it with numbers first," said Hawkhurst, " and then substitute coins."

Five minutes later, however, he exclaimed, " Hang it all ! I can't help getting the 2 in a corner. May the florin be moved from its present position ? "

" Certainly not."

" Then I give it up."

But Grigsby and I decided that we would work at it another time, so the Professor showed Hawkhurst the solution privately, and then went on with his chat.

68.—*The Postage Stamps Puzzles.*

" Now, instead of coins we'll substitute postage-stamps. Take ten current English stamps, nine of them being all of different values, and the tenth a duplicate. Stick two of them in one division and one in each of the others, so that the square shall this time add up ninepence in the eight directions as before."

" Here you are ! " cried Grigsby, after he had been scribbling for a few minutes on the back of an envelope.

The Professor smiled indulgently.

" Are you sure that there is a current English postage-stamp of the value of threepence-halfpenny ? "

" For the life of me I don't know. Isn't there ? "

" That's just like the Professor," put in Hawkhurst. " There never was such a ' tricky ' man. You never know when you have got to the bottom of his puzzles. Just when you make sure you have found a solution, he trips you up over some little point you never thought of."

" When you have done that," said the Professor, " here is a much better one for you. Stick English postage stamps so that every three divisions in a line shall add up alike, using as many stamps as you choose, so long as they are all of different values. It is a hard nut."

69.—*The Frogs and Tumblers.*

" What do you think of these ? "

The Professor brought from his capacious pockets a number of frogs, snails, lizards, and other creatures of Japanese manufacture

—very grotesque in form and brilliant in colour. While we were looking at them he asked the waiter to place sixty-four tumblers on the club table. When these had been brought and arranged in the form of a square, as shown in the illustration, he placed eight of the little green frogs on the glasses as shown.

"Now," he said, "you see these tumblers form eight horizontal and eight vertical lines, and if you look at them diagonally (both ways) there are twenty-six other lines. If you run your eye along all these forty-two lines, you will find no two frogs are anywhere in a line.

"The puzzle is this. Three of the frogs are supposed to jump from their present position to three vacant glasses, so that in their new relative positions still no two frogs shall be in a line. What are the jumps made?"

"I suppose——" began Hawkhurst.

"I know what you are going to ask," anticipated the Professor. "No; the frogs do not exchange positions, but each of the three jumps to a glass that was not previously occupied."

"But surely there must be scores of solutions?" I said.

"I shall be very glad if you can find them," replied the Professor with a dry smile. "I only know of one—or rather two, counting a reversal, which occurs in consequence of the position being symmetrical."

70.—Romeo and Juliet.

For some time we tried to make these little reptiles perform the feat allotted to them, and failed. The Professor, however, would not give away his solution, but said he would instead introduce to us a little thing that is childishly simple when you have once seen it, but cannot be mastered by everybody at the very first attempt.

"Waiter!" he called again. "Just take away these glasses, please, and bring the chessboards."

"I hope to goodness," exclaimed Grigsby, "you are not going to show us some of those awful chess problems of yours. 'White to mate Black in 427 moves without moving his pieces.' 'The bishop rooks the king, and pawns his Giuoco Piano in half a jiff.' "

" No, it is not chess. You see these two snails. They are Romeo and Juliet. Juliet is on her balcony, waiting the arrival of her love; but Romeo has been dining, and forgets, for the life of him, the number of her house. The squares represent sixty-four houses, and the amorous swain visits every house once and only once before

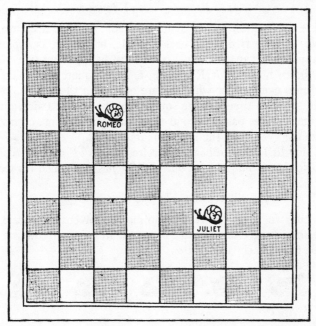

reaching his beloved. Now, make him do this with the fewest possible turnings. The snail can move up, down, and across the board and through the diagonals. Mark his track with this piece of chalk."

" Seems easy enough," said Grigsby, running the chalk along the squares. " Look ! that does it."

" Yes," said the Professor : " Romeo has got there, it is true, and visited every square once, and only once ; but you have made him turn nineteen times, and that is not doing the trick in the fewest turns possible."

Hawkhurst, curiously enough, hit on the solution at once, and the Professor remarked that this was just one of those puzzles that a person might solve at a glance or not master in six months.

71.—*Romeo's Second Journey.*

" It was a sheer stroke of luck on your part, Hawkhurst," he added. " Here is a much easier puzzle, because it is capable of more systematic analysis ; yet it may just happen that you will not do it in an hour. Put Romeo on a white square and make him crawl into every other white square once with the fewest possible turnings. This time a white square may be visited twice, but the snail must never pass a second time through the same corner of a square nor ever enter the black squares."

" May he leave the board for refreshments ? " asked Grigsby.

" No ; he is not allowed out until he has performed his feat."

72.—*The Frogs who would a-wooing go.*

While we were vainly attempting to solve this puzzle, the Professor arranged on the table ten of the frogs in two rows, as they will be found in the illustration.

" That seems entertaining," I said. " What is it ? "

" It is a little puzzle I made a year ago, and a favourite with the few people who have seen it. It is called ' The Frogs who would a-wooing go.' Four of them are supposed to go a-wooing, and after the four have each made a jump upon the table, they are in such a position that they form five straight rows with four frogs in every row."

" What's that ? " asked Hawkhurst. " I think I can do that." A few minutes later he exclaimed, " How's this ? "

" They form only four rows instead of five, and you have moved six of them," explained the Professor.

" Hawkhurst," said Grigsby severely, " you are a duffer. I see the solution at a glance. Here you are ! These two jump on their comrades' backs."

" No, no," admonished the Professor; " that is not allowed. I distinctly said that the jumps were to be made upon the table. Sometimes it passes the wit of man so to word the conditions of a problem that the quibbler will not persuade himself that he has found a flaw through which the solution may be mastered by a child of five."

After we had been vainly puzzling with these batrachian lovers for some time, the Professor revealed his secret.

The Professor gathered up his Japanese reptiles and wished us good-night with the usual seasonable compliments. We three who remained had one more pipe together, and then also left for our respective homes. Each believes that the other two racked their brains over Christmas in the determined attempt to master the Professor's puzzles; but when we next met at the club we were all unanimous in declaring that those puzzles which we had failed to solve " we really had not had time to look at," while those we had mastered after an enormous amount of labour " we had seen at the first glance directly we got home."

MISCELLANEOUS PUZZLES

73.—*The Game of Kayles.*

NEARLY all of our most popular games are of very ancient origin, though in many cases they have been considerably developed and improved. Kayles—derived from the French word *quilles*—was a great favourite in the fourteenth century, and was undoubtedly the parent of our modern game of ninepins. Kayle-pins were not confined in those days to any particular number, and they were generally made of a conical shape and set up in a straight row.

At first they were knocked down by a club that was thrown at them from a distance, which at once suggests the origin of the pastime of " shying for cocoanuts " that is to-day so popular on Bank Holidays on Hampstead Heath and elsewhere. Then the players introduced balls, as an improvement on the club.

In the illustration we get a picture of some of our fourteenth-century ancestors playing at kayle-pins in this manner.

Now, I will introduce to my readers a new game of parlour kayle-pins, that can be played across the table without any preparation whatever. You simply place in a straight row thirteen dominoes, chess-pawns, draughtsmen, counters, coins, or beans—anything will do—all close together, and then remove the second one as shown in the picture.

It is assumed that the ancient players had become so expert that they could always knock down any single kayle-pin, or any two kayle-pins that stood close together. They therefore altered the game, and it was agreed that the player who knocked down the last pin was the winner.

Therefore, in playing our table-game, all you have to do is to knock down with your fingers, or take away, any single kayle-pin

or two adjoining kayle-pins, playing alternately until one of the two players makes the last capture, and so wins. I think it will be found a fascinating little game, and I will show the secret of winning.

Remember that the second kayle-pin must be removed before you begin to play, and that if you knock down two at once those two must be close together, because in the real game the ball could not do more than this.

74.—*The Broken Chessboard.*

There is a story of Prince Henry, son of William the Conqueror, afterwards Henry I., that is so frequently recorded in the old chronicles that it is doubtless authentic. The following version of the incident is taken from Hayward's *Life of William the Conqueror,* published in 1613 :—

" Towards the end of his reigne he appointed his two sonnes Robert and Henry, with joynt authoritie, governours of Normandie ;

the one to suppresse either the insolence or levitie of the other. These went together to visit the French king lying at Constance : where, entertaining the time with varietie of disports, Henry played

with Louis, then Daulphine of France, at chesse, and did win of him very much.

"Hereat Louis beganne to growe warme in words, and was therein little respected by Henry. The great impatience of the one and the small forbearance of the other did strike in the end such a heat between them that Louis threw the chessmen at Henry's face.

" Henry again stroke Louis with the chessboard, drew blood with the blowe, and had presently slain him upon the place had he not been stayed by his brother Robert.

" Hereupon they presently went to horse, and their spurres claimed so good haste as they recovered Pontoise, albeit they were sharply pursued by the French."

Now, tradition—on this point not trustworthy—says that the chessboard broke into the thirteen fragments shown in our illustration. It will be seen that there are twelve pieces, all different in shape, each containing five squares, and one little piece of four squares only.

We thus have all the sixty-four squares of the chess-board, and the puzzle is simply to cut them out and fit them together, so as to make a perfect board properly chequered. The pieces may be easily cut out of a sheet of " squared " paper, and, if mounted on cardboard, they will form a source of perpetual amusement in the home.

If you succeed in constructing the chessboard, but do not record the arrangement, you will find it just as puzzling the next time you feel disposed to attack it.

Prince Henry himself, with all his skill and learning, would have found it an amusing pastime.

75.—*The Spider and the Fly.*

Inside a rectangular room, measuring 30 feet in length and 12 feet in width and height, a spider is at a point on the middle of

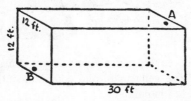

one of the end walls, 1 foot from the ceiling, as at A; and a fly is on the opposite wall, 1 foot from the floor in the centre, as shown at B. What is the shortest distance that the spider must crawl in order to reach the fly, which remains stationary ? Of course the spider never drops or uses its web, but crawls fairly.

76.—*The Perplexed Cellarman.*

Here is a little puzzle culled from the traditions of an old monastery in the west of England. Abbot Francis, it seems, was a very worthy man ; and his methods of equity extended to those little acts of charity for which he was noted for miles round.

The Abbot, moreover, had a fine taste in wines. On one occasion he sent for the cellarman, and complained that a particular bottling was not to his palate.

" Pray tell me, Brother John, how much of this wine thou didst bottle withal."

" A fair dozen in large bottles, my lord abbot, and the like in the small," replied the cellarman, " whereof five of each have been drunk in the refectory."

" So be it. There be three varlets waiting at the gate. Let the two dozen bottles be given unto them, both full and empty; and see that the dole be fairly made, so that no man receive more wine than another, nor any difference in bottles."

Poor John returned to his cellar, taking the three men with him, and then his task began to perplex him. Of full bottles he had seven large and seven small, and of empty bottles five large and five small, as shown in the illustration. How was he to make the required equitable division ?

He divided the bottles into three groups in several ways that at first sight seemed to be quite fair, since two small bottles held just the same quantity of wine as one large one. But the large bottles themselves, when empty, were not worth two small ones.

Hence the abbot's order that each man must take away the same number of bottles of each size.

Finally, the cellarman had to consult one of the monks who was good at puzzles of this kind, and who showed him how the thing was done. Can you find out just how the distribution was made ?

77.—Making a Flag.

A good dissection puzzle in so few as two pieces is rather a rarity, so perhaps the reader will be interested in the following. The diagram represents a piece of bunting, and it is required to

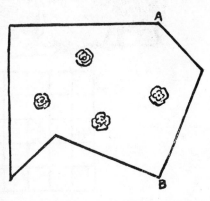

cut it into two pieces (without any waste) that will fit together and form a perfectly square flag, with the four roses symmetrically placed. This would be easy enough if it were not for the four roses, as we should merely have to cut from A to B, and insert the piece at the bottom of the flag. But we are not allowed to cut through any of the roses, and therein lies the difficulty of the puzzle. Of course we make no allowance for " turnings."

78.—*Catching the Hogs.*

In the illustration Hendrick and Katrün are seen engaged in the exhilarating sport of attempting the capture of a couple of hogs.
Why did they fail ?

Strange as it may seem, a complete answer is afforded in the little puzzle game that I will now explain.

Copy the simple diagram on a conveniently large sheet of cardboard or paper, and use four marked counters to represent the Dutchman, his wife, and the two hogs.

At the beginning of the game these must be placed on the squares on which they are shown. One player represents Hendrick and Katrün, and the other the hogs. The first player moves the Dutchman and his wife one square each in any direction (but not diagonally), and then the second player moves both pigs one square each (not diagonally) ; and so on, in turns, until Hendrick catches one hog and Katrün the other.

This you will find would be absurdly easy if the hogs moved first, but this is just what Dutch pigs will not do.

79.—*The Thirty-one Game.*

This is a game that used to be (and may be to this day, for aught I know) a favourite means of swindling employed by cardsharpers at racecourses and in railway carriages.

As, on its own merits, however, the game is particularly interesting, I will make no apology for presenting it to my readers.

The cardsharper lays down the twenty-four cards shown in the illustration, and invites the innocent wayfarer to try his luck or skill by seeing which of them can first score thirty-one, or drive his opponent beyond, in the following manner :—

One player turns down a card, say a 2, and counts " two " ; the second player turns down a card, say a 5, and, adding this to the score, counts " seven " ; the first player turns down another card, say a 1, and counts " eight " ; and so the play proceeds alternately until one of them scores the " thirty-one," and so wins.

Now, the question is, in order to win, should you turn down the first card, or courteously request your opponent to do so ? And how should you conduct your play ? The reader will perhaps say : " Oh, that is easy enough. You must play first, and turn down a 3 ; then, whatever your opponent does, he cannot stop your making ten, or stop your making seventeen, twenty-four, and the winning thirty-one.　You have only to secure these numbers to win."

But this is just that little knowledge which is such a dangerous thing, and it places you in the hands of the sharper.

You play 3, and the sharper plays 4 and counts "seven"; you play 3 and count "ten"; the sharper turns down 3 and scores "thirteen"; you play 4 and count "seventeen"; the sharper

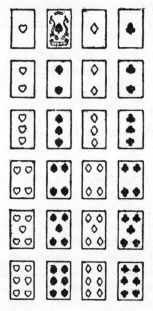

plays a 4 and counts "twenty-one"; you play 3 and make your "twenty-four."

Now the sharper plays the last 4 and scores "twenty-eight." You look in vain for another 3 with which to win, for they are all turned down!　So you are compelled either to let him make the "thirty-one" or to go yourself beyond, and so lose the game.

You thus see that your method of certainly winning breaks down utterly, by what may be called the "method of exhaustion."

I will give the key to the game, showing how you may always win; but I will not here say whether you must play first or second: you may like to find it out for yourself.

80.—*The Chinese Railways.*

Our illustration shows the plan of a Chinese city protected by pentagonal fortifications. Five European Powers were scheming and clamouring for a concession to run a railway to the place; and at last one of the Emperor's more brilliant advisers said, " Let every one of them have a concession ! " So the Celestial Govern-

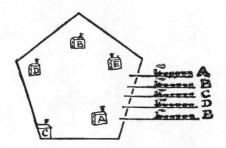

ment officials were kept busy arranging the details. The letters in the diagram show the different nationalities, and indicate not only just where each line must enter the city, but also where the station belonging to that line must be located. As it was agreed that the line of one company must never cross the line of another, the representatives of the various countries concerned were engaged so many weeks in trying to find a solution to the problem, that in the meantime a change in the Chinese Government was brought about, and the whole scheme fell through. Take your pencil and trace out the route for the line A to A, B to B, C to C, and so on, without ever allowing one line to cross another or pass through another company's station.

81.—*The Eight Clowns.*

This illustration represents a troupe of clowns I once saw on the Continent. Each clown bore one of the numbers 1 to 9 on his body. After going through the usual tumbling, juggling, and other antics, they generally concluded with a few curious little numerical

tricks, one of which was the rapid formation of a number of magic squares. It occurred to me that if clown No. 1 failed to appear (as happens in the illustration), this last item of their performance might not be so easy. The reader is asked to discover how these eight clowns may arrange themselves in the form of a square (one place being vacant), so that every one of the three columns, three rows, and each of the two diagonals shall add up the same. The vacant place may be at any part of the square, but it is No. 1 that must be absent.

82.—*The Wizard's Arithmetic.*

Once upon a time a knight went to consult a certain famous wizard. The interview had to do with an affair of the heart; but after the man of magic had foretold the most favourable issues, and concocted a love-potion that was certain to help his visitor's cause, the conversation drifted on to occult subjects generally.

" And art thou learned also in the magic of numbers? " asked the knight. " Show me but one sample of thy wit in these matters."

The old wizard took five blocks bearing numbers, and placed them on a shelf, apparently at random, so that they stood in the order 41096, as shown in our illustration. He then took in his hands an 8 and a 3, and held them together to form the number 83.

"Sir Knight, tell me," said the wizard, "canst thou multiply one number into the other in thy mind?"

"Nay, of a truth," the good knight replied. "I should need to set out upon the task with pen and scrip."

"Yet mark ye how right easy a thing it is to a man learned in the lore of far Araby, who knoweth all the magic that is hid in the philosophy of numbers!"

The wizard simply placed the 3 next to the 4 on the shelf, and the 8 at the other end. It will be found that this gives the answer quite correctly—3410968. Very curious, is it not? How many other two-figure multipliers can you find that will produce the same effect? You may place just as many blocks as you like on the shelf, bearing any figures you choose.

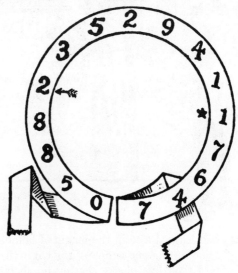

83.—*The Ribbon Problem.*

If we take the ribbon by the ends and pull it out straight, we have the number 0588235294117647. This number has the peculiarity that, if we multiply it by any one of the numbers, 2, 3, 4, 5,

6, 7, 8, or 9, we get exactly the same number in the circle, starting from a different place. For example, multiply by 4, and the product is 2352941176470588, which starts from the dart in the circle. So, if we multiply by 3, we get the same result starting from the star. Now, the puzzle is to place a different arrangement of figures on the ribbon that will produce similar results when so multiplied; only the 0 and the 7 appearing at the ends of the ribbon must not be removed.

84.—*The Japanese Ladies and the Carpet.*

Three Japanese ladies possessed a square ancestral carpet of considerable intrinsic value, but treasured also as an interesting

heirloom in the family. They decided to cut it up and make three square rugs of it, so that each should possess a share in her own house.

One lady suggested that the simplest way would be for her to take a smaller share than the other two, because then the carpet need not be cut into more than four pieces.

There are three easy ways of doing this, which I will leave the reader for the present the amusement of finding for himself, merely saying that if you suppose the carpet to be nine square feet, then one lady may take a piece two feet square whole, another a two feet square in two pieces, and the third a square foot whole.

But this generous offer would not for a moment be entertained by the other two sisters, who insisted that the square carpet should be so cut that each should get a square mat of exactly the same size.

Now, according to the best Western authorities, they would have found it necessary to cut the carpet into seven pieces; but a correspondent in Tokio assures me that the legend is that they did it in as few as six pieces, and he wants to know whether such a thing is possible.

Yes ; it can be done.

Can you cut out the six pieces that will form three square mats of equal size ?

85.—*Captain Longbow and the Bears.*

That eminent and more or less veracious traveller Captain Longbow has a great grievance with the public. He claims that during a recent expedition in Arctic regions he actually reached the North Pole, but cannot induce anybody to believe him. Of course, the difficulty in such cases is to produce proof, but he avers that future travellers, when they succeed in accomplishing the same feat, will find evidence on the spot. He says that when he got there he saw a bear going round and round the top of the pole (which he declares *is* a pole), evidently perplexed by the peculiar fact that no matter in what direction he looked it was always due south. Captain Longbow put an end to the bear's meditations by shooting him, and afterwards impaling him, in the manner shown in the

illustration, as the evidence for future travellers to which I have alluded.

When the Captain got one hundred miles south on his return journey he had a little experience that is somewhat puzzling. He was surprised one morning, on looking down from an elevation, to see no fewer than eleven bears in his immediate vicinity. But what astonished him more than anything else was the curious fact that they had so placed themselves that there were seven rows of bears, with four bears in every row. Whether or not this was the result of pure accident he cannot say, but such a thing might have happened. If the reader tries to make eleven dots on a sheet of paper so that there shall be seven rows of dots with four dots in every row, he will find some difficulty; but the captain's alleged grouping of the bears is quite possible. Can you discover how they were arranged?

86.—*The English Tour.*

This puzzle has to do with railway routes, and in these days of much travelling should prove useful. The map of England shows twenty-four towns, connected by a system of railways. A resident at the town marked A at the top of the map proposes to visit every

one of the towns once and only once, and to finish up his tour at Z. This would be easy enough if he were able to cut across country by road, as well as by rail, but he is not. How does he perform the feat ? Take your pencil and, starting from A, pass from town to town, making a dot in the towns you have visited, and see if you can end at Z.

87.—*The Chifu-Chemulpo Puzzle.*

Here is a puzzle that was once on sale in the London shops. It represents a military train—an engine and eight cars. The

puzzle is to reverse the cars, so that they shall be in the order
8, 7, 6, 5, 4, 3, 2, 1, instead of 1, 2, 3, 4, 5, 6, 7, 8, with the
engine left, as at first, on the side track.   Do this in the fewest
possible moves.   Every time the engine or a car is moved from the
main to the side track, or *vice versa*, it counts a move for each car
or engine passed over one of the points.   Moves along the main

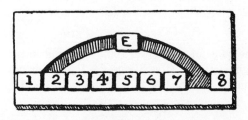

track are not counted.   With 8 at the extremity, as shown, there
is just room to pass 7 on to the side track, run 8 up to 6, and bring
down 7 again ; or you can put as many as five cars, or four and the
engine, on the siding at the same time.   The cars move without
the aid of the engine.   The purchaser is invited to " try to do it
in 20 moves."   How many do you require ?

88.—*The Eccentric Market-woman.*

Mrs. Covey, who keeps a little poultry farm in Surrey, is one
of the most eccentric women I ever met.   Her manner of doing
business is always original, and sometimes quite weird and wonderful.   She was once found explaining to a few of her choice
friends how she had disposed of her day's eggs.   She had evidently
got the idea from an old puzzle with which we are all familiar ; but
as it is an improvement on it, I have no hesitation in presenting
it to my readers.   She related that she had that day taken a
certain number of eggs to market.   She sold half of them to one
customer, and gave him half an egg over.   She next sold a third of
what she had left, and gave a third of an egg over.   She then sold
a fourth of the remainder, and gave a fourth of an egg over.   Finally,

she disposed of a fifth of the remainder, and gave a fifth of an egg over. Then what she had left she divided equally among thirteen of her friends. And, strange to say, she had not throughout all these transactions broken a single egg. Now, the puzzle is to find the smallest possible number of eggs that Mrs. Covey could have taken to market. Can you say how many ?

89.—*The Primrose Puzzle.*

Select the name of any flower that you think suitable, and that contains eight letters. Touch one of the primroses with your pencil and jump over one of the adjoining flowers to another, on

which you mark the first letter of your word. Then touch another vacant flower, and again jump over one in another direction, and write down the second letter. Continue this (taking the letters in their proper order) until all the letters have been written down, and the original word can be correctly read round the garland. You must always touch an unoccupied flower, but the flower jumped over may be occupied or not. The name of a tree may also be selected. Only English words may be used.

90.—*The Round Table.*

Seven friends, named Adams, Brooks, Cater, Dobson, Edwards, Fry, and Green, were spending fifteen days together at the seaside, and they had a round breakfast table at the hotel all to themselves. It was agreed that no man should ever sit down twice with the same two neighbours. As they can be seated, under these conditions, in just fifteen ways, the plan was quite practicable. But could the reader have prepared an arrangement for every sitting? The hotel proprietor was asked to draw up a scheme, but he miserably failed.

91.—*The Five Tea Tins.*

Sometimes people will speak of mere counting as one of the simplest operations in the world; but on occasions, as I shall show, it is far from easy. Sometimes the labour can be diminished by the use of little artifices; sometimes it is practically impossible to make the required enumeration without having a very clear head indeed. An ordinary child, buying twelve postage stamps, will almost instinctively say, when he sees there are four along one side and three along the other, "Four times three are twelve;" while his tiny brother will count them all in rows, " 1, 2, 3, 4," etc. If the child's mother has occasion to add up the numbers 1, 2, 3, up to 50, she will most probably make a long addition sum of the fifty numbers; while her husband, more used to arithmetical operations, will see at a glance that by joining the numbers at the extremes there are 25 pairs of 51; therefore, $25 \times 51 = 1{,}275$. But his smart son of twenty may go one better and say, " Why multiply by 25? Just add two 0's to the 51 and divide by 4, and there you are!"

A tea merchant has five tin tea boxes of cubical shape, which he keeps on his counter in a row, as shown in our illustration. Every box has a picture on each of its six sides, so there are thirty pictures in all ; but one picture on No. 1 is repeated on No. 4, and two other pictures on No. 4 are repeated on No. 3. There are, therefore, only twenty-seven different pictures. The owner always keeps No. 1 at one end of the row, and never allows Nos. 3 and 5 to be put side by side.

The tradesman's customer, having obtained this information,

thinks it a good puzzle to work out in how many ways the boxes may be arranged on the counter so that the order of the five pictures in front shall never be twice alike. He found the making of the count a tough little nut. Can you work out the answer without getting your brain into a tangle ? Of course, two similar pictures may be in a row, as it is all a question of their order.

92.—*The Four Porkers.*

The four pigs are so placed, each in a separate sty, that although every one of the thirty-six sties is in a straight line (either horizontally, vertically, or diagonally), with at least one of the pigs, yet no pig is in line with another. In how many different ways may the four pigs be placed to fulfil these conditions ? If you

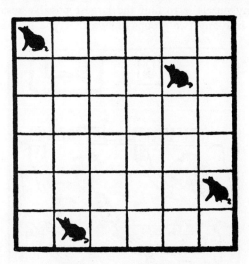

turn this page round you get three more arrangements, and if you turn it round in front of a mirror you get four more. These are not to be counted as different arrangements.

93.—*The Number Blocks.*

The children in the illustration have found that a large number of very interesting and instructive puzzles may be made out of number blocks ; that is, blocks bearing the ten digits or Arabic figures—1, 2, 3, 4, 5, 6, 7, 8, 9, and 0. The particular puzzle that they have been amusing themselves with is to divide the blocks into two groups of five, and then so arrange them in the form of two multiplication sums that one product shall be the same as the other. The number of possible solutions is very considerable, but they have hit on that arrangement that gives the smallest possible product. Thus, 3,485 multiplied by 2 is 6,970, and 6,970 multiplied by 1 is the same. You will find it quite impossible to get any smaller result.

Now, my puzzle is to find the largest possible result. Divide the blocks into any two groups of five that you like, and arrange

them to form two multiplication sums that shall produce the same product and the largest amount possible. That is all, and yet it is a nut that requires some cracking. Of course, fractions are not allowed, nor any tricks whatever. The puzzle is quite interesting enough in the simple form in which I have given it. Perhaps it should be added that the multipliers may contain two figures.

94.—*Foxes and Geese.*

Here is a little puzzle of the moving counters class that my readers will probably find entertaining. Make a diagram of any convenient size similar to that shown in our illustration, and provide six counters—three marked to represent foxes and three to represent geese. Place the geese on the discs 1, 2, and 3, and the foxes on the discs numbered 10, 11, and 12.

Now the puzzle is this. By moving one at a time, fox and goose alternately, along a straight line from one disc to the next one, try to get the foxes on 1, 2, and 3, and the geese on 10, 11, and 12—that is, make them exchange places—in the fewest possible moves.

But you must be careful never to let a fox and goose get within reach of each other, or there will be trouble. This rule, you will

find, prevents you moving the fox from 11 on the first move, as on either 4 or 6 he would be within reach of a goose. It also prevents your moving a fox from 10 to 9, or from 12 to 7. If you play 10 to 5, then your next move may be 2 to 9 with a goose, which you could not have played if the fox had not previously gone from 10. It is perhaps unnecessary to say that only one fox or one goose can be on a disc at the same time. Now, what is the smallest number of moves necessary to make the foxes and geese change places?

95.—*Robinson Crusoe's Table.*

Here is a curious extract from Robinson Crusoe's diary. It is not to be found in the modern editions of the Adventures, and is omitted in the old. This has always seemed to me to be a pity.

" The third day in the morning, the wind having abated during the night, I went down to the shore hoping to find a typewriter and other useful things washed up from the wreck of the ship; but all

that fell in my way was a piece of timber with many holes in it. My man Friday had many times said that we stood sadly in need of a square table for our afternoon tea, and I bethought me how this piece of wood might be used for that purpose. And since during the long time that Friday had now been with me I was not wanting to lay a foundation of useful knowledge in his mind, I told him that it was my wish to make the table from the timber I had found, without there being any holes in the top thereof.

" Friday was sadly put to it to say how this might be, more

especially as I said it should consist of no more than two pieces joined together; but I taught him how it could be done in such a way that the table might be as large as was possible, though, to be sure, I was amused when he said, ' My nation do much better : they stop up holes, so pieces sugars not fall through.' "

Now, the illustration gives the exact proportion of the piece of wood with the positions of the fifteen holes. How did Robinson Crusoe make the largest possible square table-top in two pieces, so that it should not have any holes in it ?

96.—*The Fifteen Orchards.*

In the county of Devon, where the cider comes from, fifteen of the inhabitants of a village are imbued with an excellent spirit of friendly rivalry, and a few years ago they decided to settle by

actual experiment a little difference of opinion as to the cultivation of apple trees. Some said they want plenty of light and air, while others stoutly maintained that they ought to be planted pretty closely, in order that they might get shade and protection from cold winds. So they agreed to plant a lot of young trees, a different number in each orchard, in order to compare results.

One man had a single tree in his field, another had two trees, another had three trees, another had four trees, another five, and so on, the last man having as many as fifteen trees in his little orchard. Last year a very curious result was found to have come about. Each of the fifteen individuals discovered that every tree in his own orchard bore exactly the same number of apples. But, what was stranger still, on comparing notes they found that the total gathered in every allotment was almost the same. In fact, if the man with eleven trees had given one apple to the man who had seven trees, and the man with fourteen trees had given three each to the men with nine and thirteen trees, they would all have had exactly the same.

Now, the puzzle is to discover how many apples each would have had (the same in every case) if that little distribution had been carried out. It is quite easy if you set to work in the right way.

97.—*The Perplexed Plumber.*

When I paid a visit to Peckham recently I found everybody asking, " What has happened to Sam Solders, the plumber ? " He seemed to be in a bad way, and his wife was seriously anxious about the state of his mind. As he had fitted up a hot-water apparatus for me some years ago which did not lead to an explosion for at least three months (and then only damaged the complexion of one of the cook's followers), I had considerable regard for him.

" There he is," said Mrs. Solders, when I called to inquire. " That's how he's been for three weeks. He hardly eats anything, and takes no rest, whilst his business is so neglected that I don't know what is going to happen to me and the five children. All day long—and night too—there he is, figuring and figuring, and tearing his hair like a mad thing. It's worrying me into an early grave."

I persuaded Mrs. Solders to explain matters to me. It seems that he had received an order from a customer to make two rectangular zinc cisterns, one with a top and the other without a top. Each was to hold exactly 1,000 cubic feet of water when filled to the brim. The price was to be a certain amount per cistern, including cost of labour. Now Mr. Solders is a thrifty man, so he naturally desired to make the two cisterns of such dimensions that

the smallest possible quantity of metal should be required. This was the little question that was so worrying him.

Can my ingenious readers find the dimensions of the most economical cistern with a top, and also the exact proportions of such a cistern without a top, each to hold 1,000 cubic feet of water? By " economical " is meant the method that requires the smallest possible quantity of metal. No margin need be allowed for what ladies would call " turnings." I shall show how I helped Mr. Solders out of his dilemma. He says : " That little wrinkle you gave me would be useful to others in my trade."

98.—*The Nelson Column.*

During a Nelson celebration I was standing in Trafalgar Square with a friend of puzzling proclivities. He had for some time been gazing at the column in an abstracted way, and seemed quite unconscious of the casual remarks that I addressed to him.

" What are you dreaming about ? " I said at last.

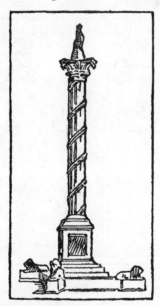

" Two feet——" he murmured.

" Somebody's Trilbys ? " I inquired.

" Five times round——"

" Two feet, five times round ! What on earth are you saying ? "

" Wait a minute," he said, beginning to figure something out on the back of an envelope. I now detected that he was in the throes of producing a new problem of some sort, for I well knew his methods of working at these things.

" Here you are ! " he suddenly exclaimed. " That's it ! A very interesting little puzzle. The height of the shaft of the Nelson column being 200 feet and its circumference 16 feet 8 inches, it is wreathed in a spiral garland which passes round it exactly five times. What is the length of the garland ? It looks rather difficult, but is really remarkably easy."

He was right. The puzzle is quite easy if properly attacked. Of course the height and circumference are not correct, but chosen for the purposes of the puzzle. The artist has also intentionally drawn the cylindrical shaft of the column of equal circumference throughout. If it were tapering, the puzzle would be less easy.

99.—*The Two Errand Boys.*

A country baker sent off his boy with a message to the butcher in the next village, and at the same time the butcher sent his boy to the baker. One ran faster than the other, and they were seen to pass at a spot 720 yards from the baker's shop. Each stopped ten minutes at his destination and then started on the return journey, when it was found that they passed each other at a spot 400 yards from the butcher's. How far apart are the two tradesmen's shops ? Of course each boy went at a uniform pace throughout.

100.—*On the Ramsgate Sands.*

Thirteen youngsters were seen dancing in a ring on the Ramsgate sands. Apparently they were playing " Round the Mulberry Bush." The puzzle is this. How many rings may they form without any child ever taking twice the hand of any other child— right hand or left ? That is, no child may ever have a second time the same neighbour.

101.—*The Three Motor-Cars.*

Pope has told us that all chance is but " direction which thou canst not see," and certainly we all occasionally come across remarkable coincidences—little things against the probability of the occurrence of which the odds are immense—that fill us with bewilderment. One of the three motor men in the illustration has just happened on one of these queer coincidences. He is pointing out to his two friends that the three numbers on their cars contain all the figures 1 to 9 and 0, and, what is more remarkable, that if the numbers on the first and second cars are multiplied together they will make the number on the third car. That is, 78, 345, and

26,910 contain all the ten figures, and 78 multiplied by 345 makes 26,910. Now, the reader will be able to find many similar sets of numbers of two, three, and five figures respectively that have the same peculiarity. But there is one set, and one only, in which the numbers have this additional peculiarity—that the second number is a multiple of the first. In other words, if 345 could be divided by 78 without a remainder, the numbers on the cars would themselves fulfil this extra condition. What are the three numbers that we want ? Remember that they must have two, three, and five figures respectively.

102.—*A Reversible Magic Square.*

Can you construct a square of sixteen different numbers so that it shall be magic (that is, adding up alike in the four rows, four columns, and two diagonals), whether you turn the diagram upside down or not ? You must not use a 3, 4, or 5, as these figures will not reverse ; but a 6 may become a 9 when reversed, a 9 a 6, a 7 a 2, and a 2 a 7. The 1, 8, and 0 will read the same both ways. Remember that the constant must not be changed by the reversal.

103.—*The Tube Railway.*

The above diagram is the plan of an underground railway. The fare is uniform for any distance, so long as you do not go twice along any portion of the line during the same journey. Now a certain passenger, with plenty of time on his hands, goes daily from A to F. How many different routes are there from which

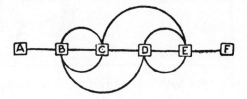

he may select ? For example, he can take the short direct route, A, B, C, D, E, F, in a straight line ; or he can go one of the long routes, such as A, B, D, C, B, C, E, D, E, F. It will be noted that he has optional lines between certain stations, and his selections of these lead to variations of the complete route. Many readers will find it a very perplexing little problem, though its conditions are so simple.

104.—*The Skipper and the Sea-Serpent.*

Mr. Simon Softleigh had spent most of his life between Tooting Bec and Fenchurch Street. His knowledge of the sea was therefore very limited. So, as he was taking a holiday on the south coast, he thought this was a splendid opportunity for picking up a little useful information. He therefore proceeded to " draw " the natives.

" I suppose," said Mr. Softleigh one morning to a jovial, weather-

beaten skipper, " you have seen many wonderful sights on the rolling seas ? "

" Bless you, sir, yes," said the skipper. " P'raps you've never seen a vanilla iceberg, or a mermaid a-hanging out her things to dry on the equatorial line, or the blue-winged shark what flies through the air in pursuit of his prey, or the sea-sarpint——"

" Have you really seen a sea-serpent ? I thought it was uncertain whether they existed."

" Uncertin ! You wouldn't say there was anything uncertin

about a sea-sarpint if once you'd seen one. The first as I seed was when I was skipper of the *Saucy Sally*. We was a-coming round Cape Horn with a cargo of shrimps from the Pacific Islands when I looks over the port side and sees a tremenjus monster like a snake, with its 'ead out of the water and its eyes flashing fire, a-bearing down on our ship. So I shouts to the bo'sun to let down the boat, while I runs below and fetches my sword—the same what I used when I killed King Chokee, the cannibal chief as eat our cabin-boy—and we pulls straight into the track of that there sea-sarpint. Well, to make a long story short, when we come alongside o' the beast I just let drive at him with that sword o' mine, and before you could say ' Tom Bowling ' I cut him into three pieces, all of exactually the same length, and afterwards we hauled 'em aboard the *Saucy Sally*. What did I do with 'em ? Well, I sold 'em to a feller in Rio Janeiro. And what do you suppose he done with 'em ? He used 'em to make tyres for his motor-car—takes a lot to puncture a sea-sarpint's skin."

" What was the length of the creature ? " asked Simon.

" Well, each piece was equal in length to three-quarters the length of a piece added to three-quarters of a cable. There's a little puzzle for you to work out, young gentleman. How many cables long must that there sea-sarpint 'ave been ? "

Now, it is not at all to the discredit of Mr. Simon Softleigh that he never succeeded in working out the correct answer to that little puzzle, for it may confidently be said that out of a thousand readers who attempt the solution not one will get it exactly right.

105.—*The Dorcas Society.*

At the close of four and a half months' hard work, the ladies of a certain Dorcas Society were so delighted with the completion of a beautiful silk patchwork quilt for the dear curate that everybody kissed everybody else, except, of course, the bashful young man himself, who only kissed his sisters, whom he had called for, to escort home. There were just a gross of osculations altogether.

How much longer would the ladies have taken over their needle-work task if the sisters of the curate referred to had played lawn tennis instead of attending the meetings? Of course we must assume that the ladies attended regularly, and I am sure that they all worked equally well. A mutual kiss here counts as two osculations.

106.—*The Adventurous Snail.*

A simple version of the puzzle of the climbing snail is familiar to everybody. We were all taught it in the nursery, and it was apparently intended to inculcate the simple moral that we should never slip if we can help it. This is the popular story. A snail

crawls up a pole 12 feet high, ascending 3 feet every day and slipping back 2 feet every night. How long does it take to get to the top? Of course, we are expected to say the answer is twelve days, because the creature makes an actual advance of 1 foot in every twenty-four hours. But the modern infant in arms is not taken in in this way. He says, correctly enough, that at the end of the ninth day the snail is 3 feet from the top, and therefore reaches the summit of its ambition on the tenth day, for it would cease to slip when it had got to the top.

Let us, however, consider the original story. Once upon a time two philosophers were walking in their garden, when one of them espied a highly respectable member of the Helix Aspersa family, a pioneer in mountaineering, in the act of making the perilous ascent of a wall 20 feet high. Judging by the trail, the gentleman calculated that the snail ascended 3 feet each day, sleeping and slipping back 2 feet every night.

" Pray tell me," said the philosopher to his friend, who was in the same line of business, " how long will it take Sir Snail to climb to the top of the wall and descend the other side ? The top of the wall, as you know, has a sharp edge, so that when he gets there he will instantly begin to descend, putting precisely the same exertion into his daily climbing down as he did in his climbing up, and sleeping and slipping at night as before."

This is the true version of the puzzle, and my readers will perhaps be interested in working out the exact number of days. Of course, in a puzzle of this kind the day is always supposed to be equally divided into twelve hours' daytime and twelve hours' night.

107.—*The Four Princes.*

The dominions of a certain Eastern monarch formed a perfectly square tract of country. It happened that the king one day discovered that his four sons were not only plotting against each other, but were in secret rebellion against himself. After consulting with his advisers he decided not to exile the princes, but to confine them to the four corners of the country, where each should be given a triangular territory of equal area, beyond the boundaries of which they would pass at the cost of their lives. Now, the royal surveyor found himself confronted by great natural difficulties, owing to the wild character of the country. The result was that while each was given exactly the same area, the four triangular districts were all of different shapes, somewhat in the manner shown in the illustration.   The puzzle is to give the three measure-

ments for each of the four districts in the smallest possible numbers —all whole furlongs.   In other words, it is required to find (in the smallest possible numbers) four rational right-angled triangles of equal area.

108.—*Plato and the Nines.*

Both in ancient and in modern times the number nine has been considered to possess peculiarly mystic qualities.   We know, for instance, that there were nine Muses, nine rivers of Hades, and that Vulcan was nine days falling down from heaven.   Then it has been confidently held that nine tailors make a man ; while we know that there are nine planets, nine days' wonders, and that a cat has nine lives—and sometimes nine tails.

Most people are acquainted with some of the curious properties of the number nine in ordinary arithmetic.   For example, write down a number containing as many figures as you like, add these figures together, and deduct the sum from the first number.   Now, the sum of the figures in this new number will always be a multiple of nine.

There was once a worthy man at Athens who was not only a cranky arithmetician, but also a mystic.   He was deeply convinced of the magic properties of the number nine, and was perpetually strolling out to the groves of Academia to bother poor old Plato with his nonsensical ideas about what he called his " lucky number." But Plato devised a way of getting rid of him.   When the seer one day proposed to inflict on him a lengthy disquisition on his favourite topic, the philosopher cut him short with the remark, " Look here, old chappie " (that is the nearest translation of the original Greek term of familiarity) : " when you can bring me the solution of this little mystery of the three nines I shall be happy to listen to your

treatise, and, in fact, record it on my phonograph for the benefit of posterity."

Plato then showed, in the manner depicted in our illustration, that three nines may be arranged so as to represent the number eleven, by putting them into the form of a fraction.   The puzzle he then propounded was so to arrange the three nines that they will represent the number twenty.

It is recorded of the old crank that, after working hard at the problem for nine years, he one day, at nine o'clock on the morning of the ninth day of the ninth month, fell down nine steps, knocked out nine teeth, and expired in nine minutes. It will be remembered that nine was his lucky number. It was evidently also Plato's.

In solving the above little puzzle, only the most elementary arithmetical signs are necessary. Though the answer is absurdly simple when you see it, many readers will have no little difficulty in discovering it. Take your pencil and see if you can arrange the three nines to represent twenty.

109.—*Noughts and Crosses.*

Every child knows how to play this game. You make a square of nine cells, and each of the two players, playing alternately, puts his mark (a nought or a cross, as the case may be) in a cell with the object of getting three in a line. Whichever player first gets three in a line wins with the exulting cry :—

> " Tit, tat, toe,
> My last go ;
> Three jolly butcher boys
> All in a row."

It is a very ancient game. But if the two players have a perfect knowledge of it, one of three things must always happen. (1) The first player should win ; (2) the first player should lose ; or (3) the game should always be drawn. Which is correct ?

110.—*Ovid's Game.*

Having examined " Noughts and Crosses," we will now consider an extension of the game that is distinctly mentioned in the works of Ovid. It is, in fact, the parent of " Nine Men's Morris," referred to by Shakespeare in *A Midsummer Night's Dream* (Act ii., Scene 2). Each player has three counters, which they play alternately on to the nine points shown in the diagram, with the object of getting three in a line and so winning. But after the six counters

are played they then proceed to move (always to an adjacent
unoccupied point) with the same object. In the example below
White played first, and Black has just played on point 7. It is now
White's move, and he will undoubtedly play from 8 to 9, and then,

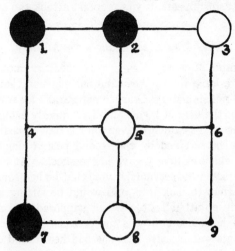

whatever Black may do, he will continue with 5 to 6, and so win.
That is the simple game. Now, if both players are equally perfect
at the game what should happen? Should the first player always
win? Or should the second player win? Or should every game
be a draw? One only of these things should always occur. Which
is it?

III.—*The Farmer's Oxen.*

A child may propose a problem that a sage cannot answer.
A farmer propounded the following question: " That ten-acre
meadow of mine will feed twelve bullocks for sixteen weeks or
eighteen bullocks for eight weeks. How many bullocks could I
feed on a forty-acre field for six weeks, the grass growing regularly
all the time? "

It will be seen that the sting lies in the tail. That steady growth of the grass is such a reasonable point to be considered, and yet to some readers it will cause considerable perplexity. The grass is, of course, assumed to be of equal length and uniform thickness in every case when the cattle begin to eat. The difficulty is not so great as it appears, if you properly attack the question.

112.—*The Great Grangemoor Mystery.*

Mr. Stanton Mowbray was a very wealthy man, a reputed millionaire, residing in that beautiful old mansion that has figured so much in English history, Grangemoor Park. He was a bachelor, spent most of the year at home, and lived quietly enough.

According to the evidence given, on the day preceding the night of the crime he received by the second post a single letter, the contents of which evidently gave him a shock. At ten o'clock at night he dismissed the servants, saying that he had some important business matters to look into, and would be sitting up late. He would require no attendance. It was supposed that after all had gone to bed he had admitted some person to the house, for one of the servants was positive that she had heard loud conversation at a very late hour.

Next morning, at a quarter to seven o'clock, one of the man-servants, on entering the room, found Mr. Mowbray lying on the floor, shot through the head, and quite dead. Now we come to the curious circumstance of the case. It was clear that after the bullet had passed out of the dead man's head it had struck the tall clock in the room, right in the very centre of the face, and actually welded together the three hands; for the clock had a seconds hand that revolved round the same dial as the hour and minute hands. But although the three hands had become welded together exactly as they stood in relation to each other at the moment of impact, yet they were free to revolve round the swivel in one piece, and had been stupidly spun round several times by the servants before Mr. Wiley Slyman was called upon the spot. But they would not move separately.

Now, inquiries by the police in the neighbourhood led to the arrest in London of a stranger who was identified by several persons as having been seen in the district the day before the murder, but it was ascertained beyond doubt at what time on the fateful morning he went away by train. If the crime took place after his departure, his innocence was established. For this and other reasons

it was of the first importance to fix the exact time of the pistol shot, the sound of which nobody in the house had heard. The clock face in the illustration shows exactly how the hands were found. Mr. Slyman was asked to give the police the benefit of his sagacity and experience, and directly he was shown the clock he smiled and said:

" The matter is supremely simple. You will notice that the three hands appear to be at equal distances from one another. The hour hand, for example, is exactly twenty minutes removed from the minute hand—that is, the third of the circumference of the dial. You attach a lot of importance to the fact that the servants have been revolving the welded hands, but their act is of no consequence whatever; for although they were welded instantaneously, as they are free on the swivel, they would swing round of themselves into equilibrium. Give me a few moments, and I can tell you beyond any doubt the exact time that the pistol was fired."

Mr. Wiley Slyman took from his pocket a notebook, and began to figure it out. In a few minutes he handed the police inspector a slip of paper, on which he had written the precise moment of the crime. The stranger was proved to be an old enemy of Mr. Mowbray's, was convicted on other evidence that was discovered; but before he paid the penalty for his wicked act, he admitted that Mr. Slyman's statement of the time was perfectly correct.

Can you also give the exact time ?

113.—*Cutting a Wood Block.*

An economical carpenter had a block of wood measuring eight inches long by four inches wide by three and three-quarter inches deep. How many pieces, each measuring two and a half inches by one inch and a half by one inch and a quarter, could he cut out of it ? It is all a question of how you cut them out. Most people would have more waste material left over than is necessary. How many pieces could you get out of the block ?

114.—*The Tramps and the Biscuits.*

Four merry tramps bought, borrowed, found, or in some other manner obtained possession of a box of biscuits, which they agreed to divide equally amongst themselves at breakfast next morning. In the night, while the others were fast asleep under the greenwood tree, one man approached the box, devoured exactly a quarter of the number of biscuits, except the odd one left over, which he threw as a bribe to their dog.   Later in the night a second man awoke and hit on the same idea, taking a quarter of what remained and giving the odd biscuit to the dog.   The third and fourth men did precisely the same in turn, taking a quarter of what they found

and giving the odd biscuit to the dog.   In the morning they divided what remained equally amongst them, and again gave the odd biscuit to the animal.   Every man noticed the reduction in the contents of the box, but, believing himself to be alone responsible, made no comments.   What is the smallest possible number of biscuits that there could have been in the box when they first acquired it ?

SOLUTIONS

THE CANTERBURY PUZZLES

1.—*The Reve's Puzzle.*

THE 8 cheeses can be removed in 33 moves, 10 cheeses in 49 moves, and 21 cheeses in 321 moves. I will give my general method of solution in the cases of 3, 4, and 5 stools.

Write out the following table to any required length :—

Stools.	Number of Cheeses.							
3	1	2	3	4	5	6	7	Natural Numbers.
4	1	3	6	10	15	21	28	Triangular Numbers.
5	1	4	10	20	35	56	84	Triangular Pyramids.
	Number of Moves.							
3	1	3	7	15	31	63	127	
4	1	5	17	49	129	321	769	
5	1	7	31	111	351	1023	2815	

The first row contains the natural numbers. The second row is found by adding the natural numbers together from the beginning. The numbers in the third row are obtained by adding together the numbers in the second row from the beginning. The fourth row contains the successive powers of 2, less 1. The next series is found by doubling in turn each number of that series and adding the number that stands above the place where you write the result. The last row is obtained in the same way. This table will at once give solutions for any number of cheeses with three stools, for triangular numbers with four stools, and for pyramidal numbers with five stools. In these cases there is always only one method of solution—that is, of piling the cheeses.

In the case of three stools, the first and fourth rows tell us that 4 cheeses may be removed in 15 moves, 5 in 31, 7 in 127. The second and fifth rows show that, with four stools, 10 may be removed in 49, and 21 in 321 moves. Also, with five stools, we find from the third and sixth rows that 20 cheeses require 111 moves, and 35 cheeses 351 moves. But we also learn from the table the necessary method of piling. Thus, with four stools and 10 cheeses, the previous column shows that we must make piles of 6 and 3, which will take 17 and 7 moves respectively—that is, we first pile the six smallest cheeses in 17 moves on one stool; then we pile the next 3 cheeses on another stool in 7 moves; then remove the largest cheese in 1 move; then replace the 3 in 7 moves; and finally replace the 6 in 17: making in all the necessary 49 moves. Similarly we are told that with five stools 35 cheeses must form piles of 20, 10, and 4, which will respectively take 111, 49, and 15 moves.

If the number of cheeses in the case of four stools is not triangular, and in the case of five stools pyramidal, then there will be more than one way of making the piles, and subsidiary tables will be required. This is the case with the Reve's 8 cheeses. But I will leave the reader to work out for himself the extension of the problem.

2.—*The Pardoner's Puzzle.*

The diagram on page 165 will show how the Pardoner started from the large black town and visited all the other towns once, and once only, in fifteen straight pilgrimages.

See No. 320, "The Rook's Tour," in *A. in M.*

3.—*The Miller's Puzzle.*

The way to arrange the sacks of flour is as follows :—2, 78, 156, 39, 4. Here each pair when multiplied by its single neighbour makes the number in the middle, and only five of the sacks need

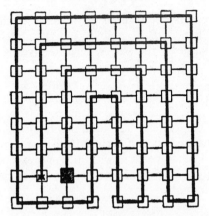

be moved. There are just three other ways in which they might have been arranged (4, 39, 156, 78, 2; or 3, 58, 174, 29, 6; or 6, 29, 174, 58, 3), but they all require the moving of seven sacks.

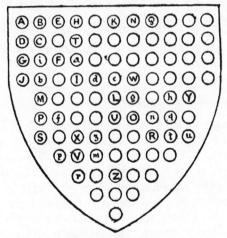

4.—*The Knight's Puzzle.*

The Knight declared that as many as 575 squares could be marked off on his shield, with a rose at every corner. How this result is achieved may be realized by reference to the accompanying diagram :—Join A, B, C, and D, and there are 66 squares of this size to be formed ; the size A, E, F, G gives 48 ; A, H, I, J, 32 ; B, K, L, M, 19 ; B, N, O, P, 10 ; B, Q, R, S, 4 ; E, T, F, C, 57 ; I, U, V, P, 33 ; H, W, X, J, 15 ; K, Y, Z, M, 3 ; E, a, b, D, 82 ; H, d, M, D, 56 ; H, e, f, G, 42 ; K, g, f, C, 32 ; N, h, z, F, 24 ; K, h, m, b, 14 ; K, O, S, D, 16 ; K, n, p, G, 10 ; K, q, r, J, 6 ; Q, t, p, C, 4 ; Q, u, r, i, 2. The total number is thus 575. These groups have been treated as if each of them represented a different sized square. This is correct, with the one exception that the squares of the form B, N, O, P are exactly the same size as those of the form K, h, m, b.

5.—*The Wife of Bath's Riddles.*

The good lady explained that a bung that is made fast in a barrel is like another bung that is falling out of a barrel because one of them is *in secure* and the other is also *insecure*. The little relationship poser is readily understood when we are told that the parental command came from the father (who was also in the room) and not from the mother.

6.—*The Host's Puzzle.*

The puzzle propounded by the jovial host of the " Tabard " Inn of Southwark had proved more popular than any other of the whole collection. " I see, my merry masters," he cried, " that I have sorely twisted thy brains by my little piece of craft. Yet it is but a simple matter for me to put a true pint of fine old ale in each of these two measures, albeit one is of five pints and the other of three pints, without using any other measure whatever."

The host of the " Tabard " Inn thereupon proceeded to explain to the pilgrims how this apparently impossible task could be done. He first filled the 5-pint and 3-pint measures, and then, turning the tap, allowed the barrel to run to waste—a proceeding against which the company protested; but the wily man showed that he was aware that the cask did not contain much more than eight pints of ale. The contents, however, do not affect the solution of the puzzle. He then closed the tap and emptied the 3-pint into the barrel; filled the 3-pint from the 5-pint; emptied the 3-pint into the barrel; transferred the two pints from the 5-pint to the 3-pint; filled the 5-pint from the barrel, leaving one pint now in the barrel; filled 3-pint from 5-pint; allowed the company to drink the contents of the 3-pint; filled the 3-pint from the 5-pint, leaving one pint now in the 5-pint; drank the contents of the 3-pint; and finally drew off one pint from the barrel into the 3-pint. He had thus obtained the required one pint of ale in each measure, to the great astonishment of the admiring crowd of pilgrims.

7.—Clerk of Oxenford's Puzzle.

The illustration shows how the square is to be cut into four pieces, and how these pieces are to be put together again to make

a magic square. It will be found that the four columns, four rows, and two long diagonals now add up to 34 in every case.

8.—The Tapiser's Puzzle.

The piece of tapestry had to be cut along the lines into three pieces so as to fit together and form a perfect square, with the pattern properly matched. It was also stipulated in effect that one of the three pieces must be as small as possible. The illustration

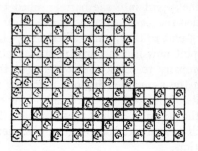 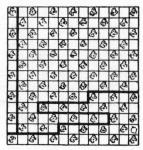

shows how to make the cuts and how to put the pieces together, while one of the pieces contains only twelve of the little squares.

9.—*The Carpenter's Puzzle.*

The carpenter said that he made a box whose internal dimensions were exactly the same as the original block of wood—that is, 3 feet by 1 foot by 1 foot. He then placed the carved pillar in this box and filled up all the vacant space with a fine, dry sand, which he carefully shook down until he could get no more into the box. Then he removed the pillar, taking great care not to lose any of the sand, which, on being shaken down alone in the box, filled a space equal to one cubic foot. This was, therefore, the quantity of wood that had been cut away.

10.—*The Puzzle of the Squire's Yeoman.*

The illustration will show how three of the arrows were removed each to a neighbouring square on the signboard of the " Chequers " Inn, so that still no arrow was in line with another. The black dots indicate the squares on which the three arrows originally stood.

11.—The Nun's Puzzle.

As there are eighteen cards bearing the letters "CANTERBURY PILGRIMS," write the numbers 1 to 18 in a circle, as shown in the diagram. Then write the first letter C against 1, and each

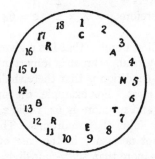

successive letter against the second number that happens to be vacant. This has been done as far as the second R. If the reader completes the process by placing Y against 2, P against 6, I against 10, and so on, he will get the letters all placed in the following order :—CYASNPTREIRMBLUIRG, which is the required arrangement for the cards, C being at the top of the pack and G at the bottom.

12.—*The Merchant's Puzzle.*

This puzzle amounts to finding the smallest possible number that has exactly sixty-four divisors, counting 1 and the number itself as divisors. The least number is 7,560. The pilgrims might, therefore, have ridden in single file, two and two, three and three, four and four, and so on, in exactly sixty-four different ways, the last manner being in a single row of 7,560.

The Merchant was careful to say that they were going over a common, and not to mention its size, for it certainly would not be possible along an ordinary road !

To find how many different numbers will divide a given number, N, let $N = a^p_1 \ b^q \ c^r \ . \ . \ .$, where $a, b, c \ . \ . \ .$ are prime numbers. Then the number of divisors will be $(p + 1) \ (q + 1) \ (r + 1) \ . \ . \ .$, which includes as divisors 1 and N itself. Thus in the case of my puzzle—

$$7,560 = 2^3 \times 3^3 \times 5 \times 7$$
$$\text{Powers} = 3 \quad 3 \quad 1 \quad 1$$
$$\text{Therefore } 4 \times 4 \times 2 \times 2 = 64 \text{ divisors.}$$

To find the smallest number that has a given number of divisors we must proceed by trial. But it is important sometimes to note whether or not the condition is that there shall be a given number of divisors *and no more.* For example, the smallest number that has seven divisors and no more is 64, while 24 has eight divisors, and might equally fulfil the conditions. The stipulation as to " no more " was not necessary in the case of my puzzle, for no smaller number has more than sixty-four divisors.

13.—*The Man of Law's Puzzle.*

The fewest possible moves for getting the prisoners into their dungeons in the required numerical order are twenty-six. The men move in the following order :—1, 2, 3, 1, 2, 6, 5, 3, 1, 2, 6, 5, 3, 1, 2, 4, 8, 7, 1, 2, 4, 8, 7, 4, 5, 6. As there are never more than one vacant dungeon to be moved into, there can be no ambiguity in the notation.

The diagram may be simplified by my " buttons and string "

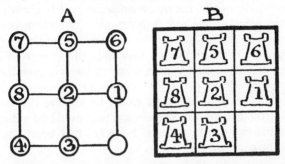

method, fully explained in *A. in M.*, p. 230. It then takes one of the simple forms of A or B, and the solution is much easier. In A we use counters ; in B we can employ rooks on a corner of a chessboard. In both cases we have to get the order $\begin{Bmatrix} 1\ 2\ 3 \\ 4\ 5\ 6 \\ 7\ 8 \end{Bmatrix}$ in the fewest possible moves.

See also solution to No. 94.

14.—*The Weaver's Puzzle.*

The illustration shows clearly how the Weaver cut his square of beautiful cloth into four pieces of exactly the same size and shape, so that each piece contained an embroidered lion and castle unmutilated in any way.

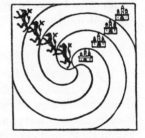

15.—*The Cook's Puzzle.*

There were four portions of warden pie and four portions of venison pasty to be distributed among eight out of eleven guests. But five out of the eleven will only eat the pie, four will only eat the pasty, and two are willing to eat of either. Any possible combination must fall into one of the following groups. (i.) Where the warden pie is distributed entirely among the five first mentioned; (ii.) where only one of the accommodating pair is given pie; (iii.) where the other of the pair is given pie; (iv.) where both of the pair are given pie. The numbers of combinations are: (i.) = 75, (ii.) = 50, (iii.) = 10, (iv.) = 10—making in all 145 ways of selecting the eight participants. A great many people will give the answer as 185, by overlooking the fact that in forty cases in class (iii.) precisely the same eight guests would be sharing the meal as in class (ii.), though the accommodating pair would be eating differently of the two dishes. This is the point that upset the calculations of the company.

16.—*The Sompnour's Puzzle.*

The number that the Sompnour confided to the Wife of Bath was twenty-nine, and she was told to begin her count at the Doctor of Physic, who will be seen in the illustration standing the second on her right. The first count of twenty-nine falls on the Shipman, who steps out of the ring. The second count falls on the Doctor, who next steps out. The remaining three counts fall respectively on the Cook, the Sompnour, and the Miller. The ladies would, therefore, have been left in possession had it not been for the unfortunate error of the good Wife. Any multiple of 2,520 added to 29 would also have served the same purpose, beginning the count at the Doctor.

17.—*The Monk's Puzzle.*

The Monk might have placed dogs in the kennels in two thousand nine hundred and twenty-six different ways, so that there should be ten dogs on every side. The number of dogs might vary from twenty to forty, and as long as the Monk kept his animals within these limits the thing was always possible.

The general solution to this puzzle is difficult. I find that for n dogs on every side of the square, the number of different ways is $\dfrac{n^4 + 10n^3 + 38n^2 + 62n + 33}{48}$, where n is odd, and $\dfrac{n^4 + 10n^3 + 38n^2 + 68n}{48} + 1$, where n is even, if we count only those arrangements that are fundamentally different. But if we count all reversals and reflections as different, as the Monk himself did, then n dogs (odd or even) may be placed in $\dfrac{n^4 + 6n^3 + 14n^2 + 15n}{6} + 1$ ways. In order that there may be n dogs on every side, the number must not be less than $2n$ nor greater than $4n$, but it may be any number within these limits.

An extension of the principle involved in this puzzle is given in No. 42, "The Riddle of the Pilgrims." See also "The Eight Villas" and "A Dormitory Puzzle" in *A. in M.*

18.—*The Shipman's Puzzle.*

There are just two hundred and sixty-four different ways in which the ship *Magdalen* might have made her ten annual voyages without ever going over the same course twice in a year. Every year she must necessarily end her tenth voyage at the island from which she first set out.

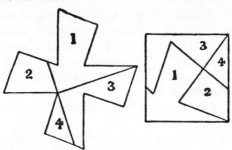

19.—*The Puzzle of the Prioress.*

The Abbot of Chertsey was quite correct. The curiously-shaped cross may be cut into four pieces that will fit together and form a perfect square. How this is done is shown in the illustration.

See also p. 31 in *A. in M.*

20.—*The Puzzle of the Doctor of Physic.*

Here we have indeed a knotty problem. Our text-books tell us that all spheres are similar, and that similar solids are as the cubes of corresponding lengths. Therefore, as the circumferences of the two phials were one foot and two feet respectively and the cubes of one and two added together make nine, what we have to find is two other numbers whose cubes added together make nine. These numbers clearly must be fractional. Now, this little question has really engaged the attention of learned men for two hundred and fifty years; but although Peter de Fermat showed in the seventeenth century how an answer may be found in two fractions with a denominator of no fewer than twenty-one figures, not only are all the published answers, by his method, that I have seen inaccurate, but nobody has ever published the much smaller result that I now print. The cubes of $\frac{415280564497}{348671682660}$ and $\frac{676702467503}{348671682660}$ added together make exactly nine, and therefore these fractions of a foot are the measurements of the circumferences of the two phials that the Doctor required to contain the same quantity of liquid as those produced. An eminent actuary and another correspondent have taken the trouble to cube out these numbers, and they both find my result quite correct.

If the phials were one foot and three feet in circumference respectively, then an answer would be that the cubes of $\frac{63284705}{21446828}$ and $\frac{28340511}{21446828}$ added together make exactly 28. See also No. 61, " The Silver Cubes."

Given a known case for the expression of a number as the sum or difference of two cubes, we can, by formula, derive from it an infinite number of other cases alternately positive and negative. Thus Fermat, starting from the known case $1^3 + 2^3 = 9$ (which we will call a fundamental case), first obtained a negative solution in bigger figures, and from this his positive solution in bigger figures still. But there is an infinite number of fundamentals, and I found by trial a negative fundamental solution in smaller figures than his derived negative solution, from which I obtained the result shown above. That is the simple explanation.

We can say of any number up to 100 whether it is possible or not to express it as the sum of two cubes, except 66. Students should read the Introduction to Lucas's *Théorie des Nombres*, p. xxx.

Some years ago I published a solution for the case of

$$6 = \left(\frac{17}{21}\right)^3 + \left(\frac{37}{21}\right)^3,$$

of which Legendre gave at some length a " proof " of impossibility; but I have since found that Lucas anticipated me in a communication to Sylvester.

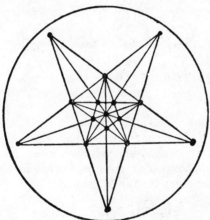

21.—*The Ploughman's Puzzle.*

The illustration shows how the sixteen trees might have been planted so as to form as many as fifteen straight rows with four trees in every row. This is in excess of what was for a long time believed to be the maximum number of rows possible; and though with our present knowledge I cannot rigorously demonstrate that fifteen rows cannot be beaten, I have a strong " pious opinion " that it is the highest number of rows obtainable.

22.—*The Franklin's Puzzle.*

The answer to this puzzle is shown in the illustration, where the numbers on the sixteen bottles all add up to 30 in the ten

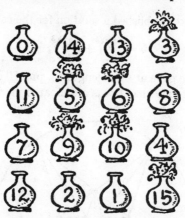

straight directions. The trick consists in the fact that, although the six bottles (3, 5, 6, 9, 10, and 15) in which the flowers have been placed are not removed, yet the sixteen need not occupy exactly the same position on the table as before. The square is, in fact, formed one step further to the left.

23.—*The Squire's Puzzle.*

The portrait may be drawn in a single line because it contains only two points at which an odd number of lines meet, but it is absolutely necessary to begin at one of these points and end at the other. One point is near the outer extremity of the King's left eye; the other is below it on the left cheek.

24.—*The Friar's Puzzle.*

The five hundred silver pennies might have been placed in the four bags, in accordance with the stated conditions, in exactly 894,348 different ways. If there had been a thousand coins there would be 7,049,112 ways. It is a difficult problem in the partition of numbers. I have a single formula for the solution of any number of coins in the case of four bags, but it was extremely hard to construct, and the best method is to find the twelve separate formulas for the different congruences to the modulus 12.

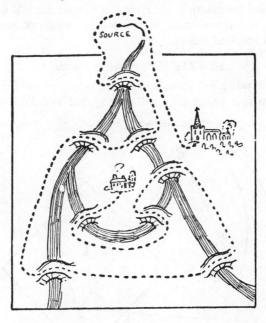

25.—*The Parson's Puzzle.*

A very little examination of the original drawing will have shown the reader that, as he will have at first read the conditions, the puzzle is quite impossible of solution. We have therefore to look for some loophole in the actual conditions as they were worded. If the Parson could get round the source of the river, he could then cross every bridge once and once only on his way to church, as shown in the annexed illustration. That this was not prohibited we shall soon find. Though the plan showed all the bridges in his parish, it only showed " part of " the parish itself. It is not stated that the river did not take its rise in the parish, and since it leads to the only possible solution, we must assume that it did. The answer would be, therefore, as shown. It should be noted that we are clearly prevented from considering the possibility of getting round the mouth of the river, because we are told it " joined the sea some hundred miles to the south," while no parish ever extended a hundred miles !

26.—*The Haberdasher's Puzzle.*

The illustration will show how the triangular piece of cloth may be cut into four pieces that will fit together and form a perfect

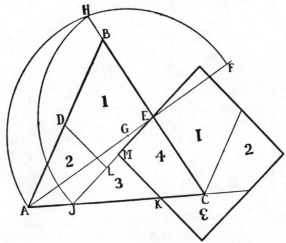

square. Bisect AB in D and BC in E ; produce the line AE to F making EF equal to EB ; bisect AF in G and describe the arc AHF; produce EB to H, and EH is the length of the side of the required square; from E with distance EH, describe the arc HJ, and make JK equal to BE; now, from the points D and K drop perpendiculars on EJ at L and M. If you have done this accurately, you will now have the required directions for the cuts.

I exhibited this problem before the Royal Society, at Burlington House, on 17th May 1905, and also at the Royal Institution in the following month, in the more general form :—" A New Problem on

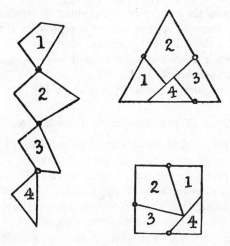

Superposition: a demonstration that an equilateral triangle can be cut into four pieces that may be reassembled to form a square, with some examples of a general method for transforming all rectilinear triangles into squares by dissection." It was also issued as a challenge to the readers of the *Daily Mail* (see issues of 1st and 8th February 1905), but though many hundreds of attempts were sent in there was not a single solver. Credit, however, is due to Mr. C. W. M'Elroy, who alone sent me the correct solution when I first published the problem in the *Weekly Dispatch* in 1902.

I add an illustration showing the puzzle in a rather curious practical form, as it was made in polished mahogany with brass hinges for use by certain audiences. It will be seen that the four pieces form a sort of chain, and that when they are closed up in one direction they form the triangle, and when closed in the other direction they form the square.

27.—*The Dyer's Puzzle.*

The correct answer is 18,816 different ways. The general formula for six fleurs-de-lys for all squares greater than 2^2 is simply this : Six times the square of the number of combinations of n things, taken three at a time, where n represents the number of fleurs-de-lys in the side of the square. Of course where n is even the remainders in rows and columns will be even, and where n is odd the remainders will be odd.

For further solution, see No. 358 in *A. in M.*

28.—*The Great Dispute between the Friar and the Sompnour.*

In this little problem we attempted to show how, by sophistical reasoning, it may apparently be proved that the diagonal of a square is of precisely the same length as two of the sides. The puzzle was to discover the fallacy, because it is a very obvious fallacy if we admit that the shortest distance between two points is a straight line. But where does the error come in ?

Well, it is perfectly true that so long as our zigzag path is formed of " steps " parallel to the sides of the square that path must be of the same length as the two sides. It does not matter if you have to use the most powerful microscope obtainable ; the rule is always true if the path is made up of steps in that way. But the error lies in the assumption that such a zigzag path can ever become a straight line. You may go on increasing the number of steps infinitely—that is, there is no limit whatever theoretically to the number of steps that can be made—but you can never reach a straight line by such a method. In fact it is just as much a " jump " to a straight line if you have a billion steps as it is at the very outset to pass from the two sides to the diagonal. It would be just as absurd to say we might go on dropping marbles into a basket until they become sovereigns as to say we can increase the number of our steps until they become a straight line. There is the whole thing in a nutshell.

29.—*Chaucer's Puzzle.*

The surface of water or other liquid is always spherical, and the greater any sphere is the less is its convexity. Hence the top diameter of any vessel at the summit of a mountain will form the base of the segment of a greater sphere than it would at the bottom. This sphere, being greater, must (from what has been already said) be less convex ; or, in other words, the spherical surface of the water must be less above the brim of the vessel, and consequently it will hold less at the top of a mountain than at the bottom. The reader is therefore free to select any mountain he likes in Italy— or elsewhere !

30.—*The Puzzle of the Canon's Yeoman.*

The number of different ways is 63,504. The general formula for such arrangements, when the number of letters in the sentence is $2n + 1$, and it is a palindrome without diagonal readings, is $[4(2^n - 1)]^2$.

I think it will be well to give here a formula for the general solution of each of the four most common forms of the diamond-letter puzzle. By the word " line " I mean the complete diagonal. Thus in A, B, C, and D, the lines respectively contain 5, 5, 7, and 9 letters. A has a non-palindrome line (the word being BOY), and the general solution for such cases, where the line contains $2n + 1$ letters, is $4(2^n - 1)$. Where the line is a single palindrome, with its middle letter in the centre, as in B, the general formula is $[4(2^n - 1)]^2$. This is the form of the Rat-catcher's Puzzle, and therefore the expression that I have given above. In cases C and D we have double palindromes, but these two represent very different types. In C, where the line contains $4n - 1$ letters, the general expression is $4(2^{2n} - 2)$. But D is by far the most difficult case of all.

I had better here state that in the diamonds under consideration (i.) no diagonal readings are allowed—these have to be dealt with specially in cases where they are possible and admitted; (ii.) readings may start anywhere; (iii.) readings may go backwards and forwards, using letters more than once in a single reading, but not the same letter twice in immediate succession. This last condition will be understood if the reader glances at C, where it is impossible to go forwards and backwards in a reading without repeating the first O touched—a proceeding which I have said is not allowed. In the case D it is very different, and this is what accounts for its greater difficulty. The formula for D is this:

$$(n + 5) \times 2^{2n+2} + \left(2^{n+2} \times \frac{1 \times 3 \times 5 \times 7 \dots (2n - 1)}{\lfloor n} \right) - 2^{n+4} - 8$$

where the number of letters in the line is $4n + 1$. In the example given there are therefore 400 readings for $n = 2$.

See also Nos. 256, 257, and 258 in *A. in M.*

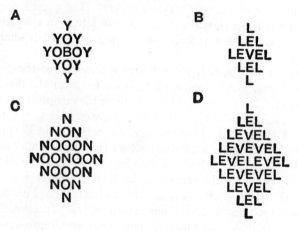

31.—*The Manciple's Puzzle.*

The simple Ploughman, who was so ridiculed for his opinion, was perfectly correct : the Miller should receive seven pieces of money, and the Weaver only one. As all three ate equal shares of the bread, it should be evident that each ate $\frac{8}{3}$ of a loaf. Therefore, as the Miller provided $\frac{15}{3}$ and ate $\frac{8}{3}$, he contributed $\frac{7}{3}$ to the Manciple's meal ; whereas the Weaver provided $\frac{9}{3}$, ate $\frac{8}{3}$, and contributed only $\frac{1}{3}$. Therefore, since they contributed to the Manciple in the proportion of 7 to 1, they must divide the eight pieces of money in the same proportion.

PUZZLING TIMES AT SOLVAMHALL CASTLE

SIR HUGH EXPLAINS HIS PROBLEMS

THE friends of Sir Hugh de Fortibus were so perplexed over many of his strange puzzles that at a gathering of his kinsmen and retainers he undertook to explain his posers.

"Of a truth," said he, "some of the riddles that I have put

forth would greatly tax the wit of the unlettered knave to rede; yet will I try to show the manner thereof in such way that all may have understanding. For many there be who cannot of themselves do all these things, but will yet study them to their gain when they be given the answers, and will take pleasure therein."

32.—*The Game of Bandy-Ball.*

Sir Hugh explained, in answer to this puzzle, that as the nine holes were 300, 250, 200, 325, 275, 350, 225, 375, and 400 yards apart, if a man could always strike the ball in a perfectly straight line and send it at will a distance of either 125 yards or 100 yards, he might go round the whole course in 26 strokes. This is clearly correct, for if we call the 125 stroke the "drive" and the 100 stroke the "approach," he could play as follows :—The first hole could be reached in 3 approaches, the second in 2 drives, the third in 2 approaches, the fourth in 2 approaches and 1 drive, the fifth in 3 drives and 1 backward approach, the sixth in 2 drives and 1 approach, the seventh in 1 drive and 1 approach, the eighth in 3 drives, and the ninth hole in 4 approaches. There are thus 26 strokes in all, and the feat cannot be performed in fewer.

33.—*Tilting at the Ring.*

"By my halidame !" exclaimed Sir Hugh, "if some of yon varlets had been put in chains, which for their sins they do truly

deserve, then would they well know, mayhap, that the length of any chain having like rings is equal to the inner width of a ring multiplied by the number of rings and added to twice the thickness of the iron whereof it is made. It may be shown that the inner width of the rings used in the tilting was one inch and two-thirds thereof, and the number of rings Stephen Malet did win was three, and those that fell to Henry de Gournay would be nine."

The knight was quite correct, for $1\frac{2}{3}$ in. $\times$ 3 $+$ 1 in. $=$ 6 in., and $1\frac{2}{3}$ in. $\times$ 9 $+$ 1 in. $=$ 16 in. Thus De Gournay beat Malet by six rings. The drawing showing the rings may assist the reader in verifying the answer and help him to see why the inner width of a link multiplied by the number of links and added to twice the thickness of the iron gives the exact length. It will be noticed that every link put on the chain loses a length equal to twice the thickness of the iron.

34.—*The Noble Demoiselle.*

" Some here have asked me," continued Sir Hugh, " how they may find the cell in the Dungeon of the Death's-head wherein the noble maiden was cast. Beshrew me ! but 'tis easy withal when you do but know how to do it. In attempting to pass through

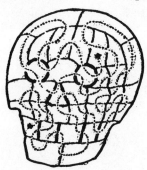

every door once, and never more, you must take heed that every cell hath two doors or four, which be even numbers, except two cells, which have but three. Now, certes, you cannot go in and out of any place, passing through all the doors once and no more, if the number of doors be an odd number. But as there be but two such odd cells, yet may we, by beginning at the one and ending at the other, so make our journey in many ways with success. I pray you, albeit, to mark that only one of these odd cells lieth on the outside of the dungeon, so we must perforce start therefrom. Marry, then, my masters, the noble demoiselle must needs have been wasting in the other."

The drawing will make this quite clear to the reader. The two " odd cells " are indicated by the stars, and one of the many routes that will solve the puzzle is shown by the dotted line. It is perfectly certain that you must start at the lower star and end at the upper one ; therefore the cell with the star situated over the left eye must be the one sought.

35.—*The Archery Butt.*

" It hath been said that the proof of a pudding is ever in the eating thereof, and by the teeth of Saint George I know no better

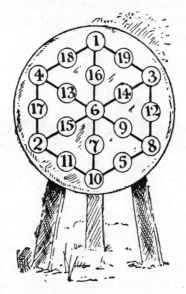

way of showing how this placing of the figures may be done than by the doing of it. Therefore have I in suchwise written the numbers that they do add up to twenty and three in all the twelve lines of three that are upon the butt."

I think it well here to supplement the solution of De Fortibus with a few remarks of my own. The nineteen numbers may be so arranged that the lines will add up to any number we may choose to select from 22 to 38 inclusive, excepting 30. In some cases there are several different solutions, but in the case of 23 there are only two. I give one of these. To obtain the second solution exchange respectively 7, 10, 5, 8, 9, in the illustration, with 13, 4, 17, 2, 15. Also exchange 18 with 12, and the other numbers may remain unmoved. In every instance there must be an even number in the central place, and any such number from 2 to 18 may occur. Every solution has its complementary. Thus, if for every number in the accompanying drawing we substitute the difference between it and 20, we get the solution in the case of 37. Similarly, from the arrangement in the original drawing, we may at once obtain a solution for the case of 38.

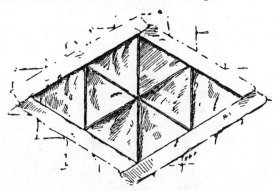

36.—*The Donjon Keep Window.*

In this case Sir Hugh had greatly perplexed his chief builder by demanding that he should make a window measuring one foot on every side and divided by bars into eight lights, having all their sides equal. The illustration will show how this was to be done. It will be seen that if each side of the window measures one foot, then each of the eight triangular lights is six inches on every side.

" Of a truth, master builder," said De Fortibus slyly to the architect, " I did not tell thee that the window must be square, as it is most certain it never could be."

37.—*The Crescent and the Cross.*

" By the toes of St. Moden," exclaimed Sir Hugh de Fortibus when this puzzle was brought up, " my poor wit hath never shaped a more cunning artifice or any more bewitching to look upon. It came to me as in a vision, and ofttimes have I marvelled at the

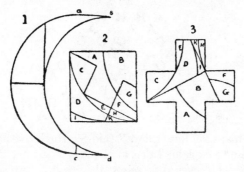

thing, seeing its exceeding difficulty. My masters and kinsmen, it is done in this wise."

The worthy knight then pointed out that the crescent was of a particular and somewhat irregular form—the two distances *a* to *b* and *c* to *d* being straight lines, and the arcs *ac* and *bd* being precisely similar. He showed that if the cuts be made as in Figure 1, the four pieces will fit together and form a perfect square, as shown in Figure 2, if we there only regard the three curved lines. By now making the straight cuts also shown in Figure 2, we get the ten pieces that fit together, as in Figure 3, and form a perfectly symmetrical Greek cross. The proportions of the crescent and the cross in the original illustration were correct, and the solution can be demonstrated to be absolutely exact and not merely approximate.

I have a solution in considerably fewer pieces, but it is far more difficult to understand than the above method, in which the problem is simplified by introducing the intermediate square.

38.—*The Amulet.*

The puzzle was to place your pencil on the A at the top of the amulet and count in how many different ways you could trace out the word " Abracadabra " downwards, always passing from a letter to an adjoining one.

" Now, mark ye, fine fellows," said Sir Hugh to some who had besought him to explain, " that at the very first start there be two ways open : whichever B ye select, there will be two several ways of proceeding (twice times two are four) ; whichever R ye select, there be two ways of going on (twice times four are eight) ; and so on until the end.   Each letter in order from A downwards may so be reached in 2, 4, 8, 16, 32, etc., ways.   Therefore, as there be ten lines or steps in all from A to the bottom, all ye need do is to multiply ten 2's together, and truly the result, 1024, is the answer thou dost seek."

39.—*The Snail on the Flagstaff.*

Though there was no need to take down and measure the staff, it is undoubtedly necessary to find its height before the answer

can be given. It was well known among the friends and retainers
of Sir Hugh de Fortibus that he was exactly six feet in height.
It will be seen in the original picture that Sir Hugh's height is just
twice the length of his shadow. Therefore we all know that the
flagstaff will, at the same place and time of day, be also just twice
as long as its shadow. The shadow of the staff is the same length
as Sir Hugh's height ; therefore this shadow is six feet long, and
the flagstaff must be twelve feet high. Now, the snail, by climbing
up three feet in the daytime and slipping back two feet by night,
really advances one foot in a day of twenty-four hours. At the
end of nine days it is three feet from the top, so that it reaches its
journey's end on the tenth day.

The reader will doubtless here exclaim, " This is all very well ;
but how were we to know the height of Sir Hugh ? It was never
stated how tall he was ! " No, it was not stated in so many words,
but it was none the less clearly indicated to the reader who is sharp
in these matters. In the original illustration to the donjon keep
window Sir Hugh is shown standing against a wall, the window in
which is stated to be one foot square on the inside. Therefore, as
his height will be found by measurement to be just six times the
inside height of the window, he evidently stands just six feet in
his boots !

40.—*Lady Isabel's Casket.*

The last puzzle was undoubtedly a hard nut, but perhaps difficulty does not make a good puzzle any the less interesting when
we are shown the solution. The accompanying diagram indicates
exactly how the top of Lady Isabel de Fitzarnulph's casket was
inlaid with square pieces of rare wood (no two squares alike) and
the strip of gold 10 inches by a quarter of an inch. This is the
only possible solution, and it is a singular fact (though I cannot
here show the subtle method of working) that the number, sizes,
and order of those squares are determined by the given dimensions
of the strip of gold, and the casket can have no other dimensions
than 20 inches square. The number in a square indicates the length

in inches of the side of that square, so the accuracy of the answer can be checked almost at a glance.

Sir Hugh de Fortibus made some general concluding remarks on the occasion that are not altogether uninteresting to-day.

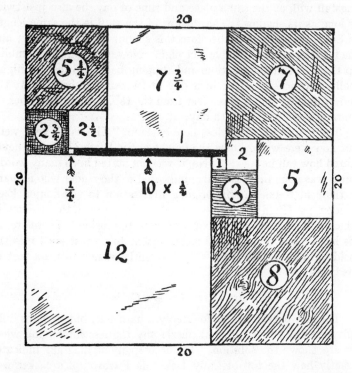

" Friends and retainers," he said, " if the strange offspring of my poor wit about which we have held pleasant counsel to-night hath mayhap had some small interest for ye, let these matters serve to call to mind the lesson that our fleeting life is rounded and beset with enigmas. Whence we came and whither we go be riddles, and albeit such as these we may never bring within our understanding, yet there be many others with which we and they that do come after us will ever strive for the answer. Whether success do attend or do not attend our labour, it is well that we make the attempt; for 'tis truly good and honourable to train the mind, and the wit, and the fancy of man, for out of such doth issue all manner of good in ways unforeseen for them that do come after us."

THE MERRY MONKS OF RIDDLEWELL

41.—*The Riddle of the Fish-pond.*

NUMBER the fish baskets in the illustration from 1 to 12 in the direction that Brother Jonathan is seen to be going. Starting from 1, proceed as follows, where " 1 to 4 " means, take the fish from basket No. 1 and transfer it to basket No. 4 :—

1 to 4, 5 to 8, 9 to 12, 3 to 6, 7 to 10, 11 to 2, and complete the last revolution to 1, making three revolutions in all. Or you can proceed this way :—

4 to 7, 8 to 11, 12 to 3, 2 to 5, 6 to 9, 10 to 1.

It is easy to solve in four revolutions, but the solutions in three are more difficult to discover.

42.—*The Riddle of the Pilgrims.*

If it were not for the Abbot's conditions that the number of guests in any room may not exceed three, and that every room must be occupied, it would have been possible to accommodate either 24, 27, 30, 33, 36, 39, or 42 pilgrims. But to accommodate 24 pilgrims so that there shall be twice as many sleeping on the upper floor as on the lower floor, and eleven persons on each side of the building, it will be found necessary to leave some of the rooms empty. If, on the other hand, we try to put up 33, 36, 39 or 42 pilgrims, we shall find that in every case we are obliged to place more than three persons in some of the rooms. Thus we know that the number of pilgrims originally announced (whom, it will be remembered, it was possible to accommodate under the conditions of the Abbot) must have been 27, and that, since three more than this number were actually provided with beds, the total number of pilgrims was 30. The accompanying diagram shows

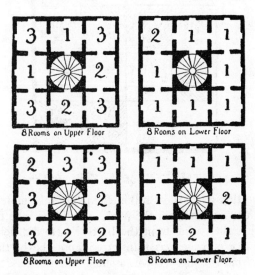

8 Rooms on Upper Floor

8 Rooms on Lower Floor

8 Rooms on Upper Floor

8 Rooms on Lower Floor.

how they might be arranged, and if in each instance we regard the upper floor as placed above the lower one, it will be seen that there are eleven persons on each side of the building, and twice as many above as below.

43.—*The Riddle of the Tiled Hearth.*

The correct answer is shown in the illustration on page 196. No tile is in line (either horizontally, vertically, or diagonally) with another tile of the same design, and only three plain tiles are used. If after placing the four lions you fall into the error of placing four other tiles of another pattern, instead of only three, you will be left with four places that must be occupied by plain tiles. The secret consists in placing four of one kind and only three of each of the others.

44.—The Riddle of the Sack of Wine.

The question was: Did Brother Benjamin take more wine from the bottle than water from the jug? Or did he take more water from the jug than wine from the bottle? He did neither. The same quantity of wine was transferred from the bottle as water was taken from the jug. Let us assume that the glass would hold a quarter of a pint. There was a pint of wine in the bottle and a pint of water in the jug. After the first manipulation the bottle contains three-quarters of a pint of wine, and the jug one pint of water mixed with a quarter of a pint of wine. Now, the second transaction consists in taking away a fifth of the contents of the jug—that is, one-fifth of a pint of water mixed with one-fifth of a quarter of a pint of wine. We thus leave behind in the jug four-fifths of a quarter of a pint of wine—that is, one-fifth of a pint—while we transfer from the jug to the bottle an equal quantity (one-fifth of a pint) of water.

45.—The Riddle of the Cellarer.

There were 100 pints of wine in the cask, and on thirty occasions John the Cellarer had stolen a pint and replaced it with a pint of water. After the first theft the wine left in the cask would be

99 pints; after the second theft the wine in the cask would be $\frac{9801}{100}$ pints (the square of 99 divided by 100); after the third theft there would remain $\frac{970299}{10000}$ (the cube of 99 divided by the square of 100); after the fourth theft there would remain the fourth power of 99 divided by the cube of 100; and after the thirtieth theft there would remain in the cask the thirtieth power of 99 divided by the twenty-ninth power of 100. This by the ordinary method of calculation gives us a number composed of 59 figures to be divided by a number composed of 58 figures! But by the use of logarithms it may be quickly ascertained that the required quantity is very nearly $73\frac{97}{100}$ pints of wine left in the cask. Consequently the cellarer stole nearly 26.03 pints. The monks doubtless omitted the answer for the reason that they had no tables of logarithms, and did not care to face the task of making that long and tedious calculation in order to get the quantity " to a nicety," as the wily cellarer had stipulated.

By a simplified process of calculation, I have ascertained that the exact quantity of wine stolen would be

$$26.0299626611719577269984907683285057747323737647323555565\overline{2999}$$

pints. A man who would involve the monastery in a fraction of fifty-eight decimals deserved severe punishment.

46.—*The Riddle of the Crusaders.*

The correct answer is that there would have been 602,176 Crusaders, who could form themselves into a square 776 by 776; and after the stranger joined their ranks, they could form 113 squares of 5,329 men—that is, 73 by 73. Or $113 \times 73^2 - 1 = 776^2$. This is a particular case of the so-called " Pellian Equation," respecting which see *A. in M.*, p. 164.

47.—*The Riddle of St. Edmondsbury.*

The reader is aware that there are prime numbers and composite whole numbers. Now, 1,111,111 cannot be a prime number, because if it were the only possible answers would be those proposed by Brother Benjamin and rejected by Father Peter. Also it cannot have more than two factors, or the answer would be indeterminate. As a matter of fact, 1,111,111 equals 239 × 4649 (both primes), and since each cat killed more mice than there were cats, the answer must be 239 cats. See also the Introduction, p. 18.

Treated generally, this problem consists in finding the factors, if any, of numbers of the form $\dfrac{10^n - 1}{9}$.

Lucas, in his *L'Arithmétique Amusante*, gives a number of curious tables which he obtained from an arithmetical treatise, called the *Talkhys*, by Ibn Albanna, an Arabian mathematician and astronomer of the first half of the thirteenth century. In the Paris National Library are several manuscripts dealing with the *Talkhys*, and a commentary by Alkalaçadi, who died in 1486. Among the tables given by Lucas is one giving all the factors of numbers of the above form up to $n = 18$. It seems almost inconceivable that Arabians of that date could find the factors where $n = 17$, as given in my Introduction. But I read Lucas as stating that they are given in *Talkhys*, though an eminent mathematician reads him differently, and suggests to me that they were discovered by Lucas himself. This can, of course, be settled by an examination of *Talkhys*, but this has not been possible during the war.

The difficulty lies wholly with those cases where n is a prime number. If $n = 2$, we get the prime 11. The factors when $n = 3$, 5, 11, and 13 are respectively (3 . 37), (41 . 271), (21,649 . 513,239), and (53 . 79 . 265371653). I have given in these pages the factors where $n = 7$ and 17. The factors when $n = 19$, 23, and 37 are unknown, if there are any.* When $n = 29$, the factors are (3,191 . 16,763 . 43,037 .

* Mr. Oscar Hoppe, of New York, informs me that, after reading my statement in the Introduction, he was led to investigate the case of $n = 19$, and after long and tedious work he succeeded in proving the number to be a prime. He submitted his proof to the London Mathematical Society, and a specially appointed committee of that body accepted the proof as final and conclusive. He refers me to the *Proceedings* of the Society for 14th February 1918.

62,003 . 77,843,839,397) ; when $n = 31$, one factor is 2,791 ; and when $n = 41$, two factors are (83 . 1,231).

As for the even values of n, the following curious series of factors will doubtless interest the reader. The numbers in brackets are primes.

$$n = \ 2 = (11)$$
$$n = \ 6 = (11) \times 111 \qquad\qquad \times 91$$
$$n = 10 = (11) \times 11,111 \qquad\quad \times (9,091)$$
$$n = 14 = (11) \times 1,111,111 \qquad \times (909,091)$$
$$n = 18 = (11) \times 111,111,111 \times 90,909,091$$

Or we may put the factors this way :—

$$n = \ 2 = (11)$$
$$n = \ 6 = 111 \qquad\qquad\quad \times 1,001$$
$$n = 10 = 11,111 \qquad\qquad \times 100,001$$
$$n = 14 = 1,111,111 \qquad\ \times 10,000,001$$
$$n = 18 = 111,111,111 \times 1,000,000,001$$

In the above two tables n is of the form $4m + 2$. When n is of the form $4m$ the factors may be written down as follows :—

$$n = \ 4 = (11) \times (101)$$
$$n = \ 8 = (11) \times (101) \times 10,001$$
$$n = 12 = (11) \times (101) \times 100,010,001$$
$$n = 16 = (11) \times (101) \times 1,000,100,010,001.$$

When $n = 2$, we have the prime number 11 ; when $n = 3$, the factors are 3 . 37 ; when $n = 6$, they are 11 . 3 . 37 . 7 . 13 ; when $n = 9$, they are 3^2 . 37 . 333,667. Therefore we know that factors of $n = 18$ are 11 . 3^2 . 37 . 7 . 13 . 333,667, while the remaining factor is composite and can be split into 19 . 52579. This will show how the working may be simplified when n is not prime.

48.—*The Riddle of the Frogs' Ring.*

The fewest possible moves in which this puzzle can be solved are 118. I will give the complete solution. The black figures on white discs move in the directions of the hands of a clock, and the white figures on black discs the other way. The following are the numbers in the order in which they move. Whether you have to make a simple move or a leaping move will be clear from the position, as you never can have an alternative. The moves enclosed in brackets are to be played five times over : 6, 7, 8, 6, 5, 4, 7, 8, 9, 10, 6, 5, 4, 3, 2, 7, 8, 9, 10, 11 (6, 5, 4, 3, 2, 1), 6, 5, 4, 3, 2, 12, (7, 8, 9, 10, 11, 12), 7, 8, 9, 10, 11, 1, 6, 5, 4, 3, 2, 12, 7, 8, 9, 10, 11, 6, 5, 4, 3, 2, 8, 9, 10, 11, 4, 3, 2, 10, 11, 2. We thus have made 118 moves within the conditions, the black frogs have changed places with the white ones, and 1 and 12 are side by side in the positions stipulated.

The general solution in the case of this puzzle is $3n^2 + 2n - 2$ moves, where the number of frogs of each colour is n. The law governing the sequence of moves is easily discovered by an examination of the simpler cases, where $n = 2$, 3, and 4.

If, instead of 11 and 12 changing places, the 6 and 7 must interchange, the expression is $n^2 + 4n + 2$ moves. If we give n the value 6, as in the example of the Frogs' Ring, the number of moves would be 62.

For a general solution of the case where frogs of one colour reverse their order, leaving the blank space in the same position, and each frog is allowed to be moved in either direction (leaping, of course, over his own colour), see " The Grasshopper Puzzle " in *A. in M.,* p. 193.

THE STRANGE ESCAPE OF THE
KING'S JESTER

ALTHOUGH the king's jester promised that he would "thereafter make the manner thereof plain to all," there is no record of his having ever done so. I will therefore submit to the reader my own views as to the probable solutions to the mysteries involved.

49.—*The Mysterious Rope.*

When the jester "divided his rope in half," it does not follow that he cut it into two parts, each half the original length of the rope. No doubt he simply untwisted the strands, and so divided it into two ropes, each of the original length, but one-half the thickness. He would thus be able to tie the two together and make a rope nearly twice the original length, with which it is quite conceivable that he made good his escape from the dungeon.

50.—*The Underground Maze.*

How did the jester find his way out of the maze in the dark? He had simply to grope his way to a wall and then keep on walking without once removing his left hand (or right hand) from the wall. Starting from A, the dotted line will make the route clear when he goes to the left. If the reader tries the route to the right in the same way he will be equally successful; in fact, the two routes unite and cover every part of the walls of the maze except those two detached parts on the left-hand side—one piece like a

U, and the other like a distorted E.   This rule will apply to the majority of mazes and puzzle gardens; but if the centre were en-

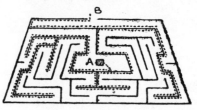

closed by an isolated wall in the form of a split ring, the jester would simply have gone round and round this ring.

See the article, "Mazes, and How to Thread Them," in *A. in M.*

51.—*The Secret Lock.*

This puzzle entailed the finding of an English word of three letters, each letter being found on a different dial.   Now, there is no English word composed of consonants alone, and the only vowel appearing anywhere on the dials is Y.   No English word begins with Y and has the two other letters consonants, and all the words of three letters ending in Y (with two consonants) either begin with an S or have H, L, or R as their second letter.   But these four consonants do not appear.   Therefore Y must occur in the middle, and the only word that I can find is " PYX," and there can be little doubt that this was the word.   At any rate, it solves our puzzle.

52.—*Crossing the Moat.*

No doubt some of my readers will smile at the statement that a man in a boat on smooth water can pull himself across with the tiller rope !   But it is a fact.   If the jester had fastened the end of his rope to the stern of the boat and then, while standing in the bows, had given a series of violent jerks, the boat would have been propelled forward.   This has often been put to a practical test, and it is said that a speed of two or three miles an hour may be attained.   See W. W. Rouse Ball's *Mathematical Recreations.*

53.—*The Royal Gardens.*

This puzzle must have struck many readers as being absolutely impossible. The jester said : " I had, of a truth, entered every one of the sixteen gardens once, and never more than once." If we follow the route shown in the accompanying diagram, we find that there is no difficulty in once entering all the gardens but one before reaching the last garden containing the exit B. The difficulty is to get into the garden with a star, because if we leave the B garden we are compelled to enter it a second time before escaping, and no garden may be entered twice. The trick consists in the

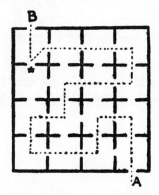

fact that you may enter that starred garden without necessarily leaving the other. If, when the jester got to the gateway where the dotted line makes a sharp bend, his intention had been to hide in the starred garden, but after he had put one foot through the doorway, upon the star, he discovered it was a false alarm and withdrew, he could truly say : " I entered the starred garden, because I put my foot and part of my body in it ; and I did not enter the other garden twice, because, after once going in I never left it until I made my exit at B." This is the only answer possible, and it was doubtless that which the jester intended.

See " The Languishing Maiden," in *A. in M.*

54.—*Bridging the Ditch.*

The solution to this puzzle is best explained by the illustration. If he had placed his eight planks, in the manner shown, across

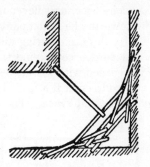

the angle of the ditch, he would have been able to cross without much trouble. The king's jester might thus have well overcome all his difficulties and got safely away, as he has told us that he succeeded in doing.

THE SQUIRE'S CHRISTMAS PUZZLE PARTY

HOW THE VARIOUS TRICKS WERE DONE

THE record of one of Squire Davidge's annual " Puzzle Parties," made by the old gentleman's young lady relative, who had often spent a merry Christmas at Stoke Courcy Hall, does not contain the solutions of the mysteries. So I will give my own answers to the puzzles and try to make them as clear as possible to those who may be more or less novices in such matters.

55.—*The Three Teacups.*

Miss Charity Lockyer clearly must have had a trick up her sleeve, and I think it highly probable that it was conceived on the following lines. She proposed that ten lumps of sugar should be placed in three teacups, so that there should be an odd

number of lumps in every cup. The illustration perhaps shows Miss Charity's answer, and the figures on the cups indicate the number of lumps that have been separately placed in them. By placing the cup that holds one lump inside the one that holds two lumps, it can be correctly stated that every cup contains an odd number of lumps. One cup holds seven lumps, another holds one lump, while the third cup holds three lumps. It is evident that if a cup contains another cup it also contains the contents of that second cup.

There are in all fifteen different solutions to this puzzle.　Here they are :—

1	0	9		1	4	5		9	0	1
3	0	7		7	0	3		7	2	1
1	2	7		5	2	3		5	4	1
5	0	5		3	4	3		3	6	1
3	2	5		1	6	3		1	8	1

The first two numbers in a triplet represent respectively the number of lumps to be placed in the inner and outer of the two cups that are placed one inside the other.　It will be noted that the outer cup of the pair may itself be empty.

56.—The Eleven Pennies.

It is rather evident that the trick in this puzzle was as follows :— From the eleven coins take five ; then add four (to those already taken away) and you leave nine—in the second heap of those removed !

57.—The Christmas Geese.

Farmer Rouse sent exactly 101 geese to market.　Jabez first sold Mr. Jasper Tyler half of the flock and half a goose over (that is, $50\frac{1}{2}+\frac{1}{2}$, or 51 geese, leaving 50) ; he then sold Farmer Avent a third of what remained and a third of a goose over (that is, $16\frac{2}{3}+\frac{1}{3}$, or 17 geese, leaving 33) ; he then sold Widow Foster a quarter of what remained and three-quarters of a goose over (that is, $8\frac{1}{4}+\frac{3}{4}$ or 9 geese, leaving 24) ; he next sold Ned Collier a fifth of what he had left and gave him a fifth of a goose " for the missus " (that is, $4\frac{4}{5}+\frac{1}{5}$, or 5 geese, leaving 19).　He then took these 19 back to his master.

58.—The Chalked Numbers.

This little jest on the part of Major Trenchard is another trick puzzle, and the face of the roguish boy on the extreme right, with the figure 9 on his back, showed clearly that he was in the secret, whatever that secret might be. I have no doubt (bearing in mind the Major's hint as to the numbers being " properly regarded ") that his answer was that depicted in the illustration, where boy No. 9 stands on his head and so converts his number into 6. This

makes the total 36—an even number—and by making boys 3 and 4 change places with 7 and 8, we get 1 2 7 8 and 5 3 4 6, the figures of which, in each case, add up to 18. There are just three other ways in which the boys may be grouped : 1 3 6 8—2 4 5 7, 1 4 6 7 —2 3 5 8, and 2 3 6 7—1 4 5

59.—*Tasting the Plum Puddings.*

The diagram will show how this puzzle is to be solved. It is the only way within the conditions laid down. Starting at the pudding with holly at the top left-hand corner, we strike out all the puddings in twenty-one straight strokes, taste the steaming hot pudding at the end of the tenth stroke, and end at the second sprig of holly.

Here we have an example of a chess rook's path that is not re-entrant, but between two squares that are at the greatest possible distance from one another. For if it were desired to move, under the condition of visiting every square once and once only, from one corner square to the other corner square on the same diagonal, the feat is impossible.

There are a good many different routes for passing from one sprig of holly to the other in the smallest possible number of moves

—twenty-one—but I have not counted them. I have recorded fourteen of these, and possibly there are more. Any one of these would serve our purpose, except for the condition that the tenth stroke shall end at the steaming hot pudding. This was intro-

duced to stop a plurality of solutions—called by the maker of chess problems " cooks." I am not aware of more than one solution to this puzzle; but as I may not have recorded all the tours, I cannot make a positive statement on the point at the time of writing.

60.—*Under the Mistletoe Bough.*

Everybody was found to have kissed everybody else once under the mistletoe, with the following additions and exceptions: No male kissed a male; no man kissed a married woman except his own wife; all the bachelors and boys kissed all the maidens and girls twice; the widower did not kiss anybody, and the widows did not kiss each other. Every kiss was returned, and the double performance was to count as one kiss. In making a list of the company, we can leave out the widower altogether, because he took no part in the osculatory exercise.

7 Married couples	14
3 Widows	3
12 Bachelors and Boys	12
10 Maidens and Girls	10
Total	39 Persons

Now, if every one of these 39 persons kissed everybody else once, the number of kisses would be 741; and if the 12 bachelors and boys each kissed the 10 maidens and girls once again, we must add 120, making a total of 861 kisses. But as no married man kissed a married woman other than his own wife, we must deduct 42 kisses; as no male kissed another male, we must deduct 171 kisses; and as no widow kissed another widow, we must deduct 3 kisses. We have, therefore, to deduct 42+171+3=216 kisses from the above total of 861, and the result, 645, represents exactly the number of kisses that were actually given under the mistletoe bough.

61.—*The Silver Cubes.*

There is no limit to the number of different dimensions that will give two cubes whose sum shall be exactly seventeen cubic inches. Here is the answer in the smallest possible numbers. One of the silver cubes must measure $2\frac{23278}{40831}$ inches along each edge, and the other must measure $\frac{11663}{40831}$ inch. If the reader likes to undertake the task of cubing each number (that is, multiply each number twice by itself), he will find that when added together the contents exactly equal seventeen cubic inches. See also No. 20, " The Puzzle of the Doctor of Physic."

THE ADVENTURES OF THE PUZZLE CLUB

62.—*The Ambiguous Photograph.*

ONE by one the members of the Club succeeded in discovering the key to the mystery of the Ambiguous Photograph, except Churton, who was at length persuaded to " give it up." Herbert Baynes then pointed out to him that the coat that Lord Marksford was carrying over his arm was a lady's coat, because the buttons are on the left side, whereas a man's coat always has the buttons on the right-hand side. Lord Marksford would not be likely to walk about the streets of Paris with a lady's coat over his arm unless he was accompanying the owner. He was therefore walking with the lady.

As they were talking a waiter brought a telegram to Baynes.

" Here you are," he said, after reading the message. " A wire from Dovey : ' Don't bother about photo. Find lady was the gentleman's sister, passing through Paris.' That settles it. You might notice that the lady was lightly clad, and therefore the coat might well be hers. But it is clear that the rain was only a sudden shower, and no doubt they were close to their destination, and she did not think it worth while to put the coat on."

63.—*The Cornish Cliff Mystery.*

Melville's explanation of the Cornish Cliff Mystery was very simple when he gave it. Yet it was an ingenious trick that the two criminals adopted, and it would have completely succeeded had not our friends from the Puzzle Club accidentally appeared on the scene. This is what happened : When Lamson and Marsh reached the stile, Marsh alone walked to the top of the cliff, with Lamson's larger boots in his hands. Arrived at the edge of the cliff, he changed the boots and walked backwards to the stile, carrying his own boots.

This little manœuvre accounts for the smaller footprints showing a deeper impression at the heel, and the larger prints a deeper impression at the toe ; for a man will walk more heavily on his heels when going forward, but will make a deeper impression with the toes in walking backwards. It will also account for the fact that the large footprints were sometimes impressed over the smaller ones, but never the reverse ; also for the circumstance that the larger footprints showed a shorter stride, for a man will necessarily take a smaller stride when walking backwards. The pocket-book was intentionally dropped, to lead the police to discover the footprints, and so be put on the wrong scent.

64.—*The Runaway Motor-Car.*

Russell found that there are just twelve five-figure numbers that have the peculiarity that the first two figures multiplied by the last three—all the figures being different, and there being no o —will produce a number with exactly the same five figures, in a different order. But only one of these twelve begins with a 1— namely, 14926. Now, if we multiply 14 by 926, the result is 12964, which contains the same five figures. The number of the motor-car was therefore 14926.

Here are the other eleven numbers :—24651, 42678, 51246, 57834, 75231, 78624, 87435, 72936, 65281, 65983, and 86251.

Compare with the problems in " Digital Puzzles," section of *A. in M.*, and with Nos. 93 and 101 in these pages.

65.—*The Mystery of Ravensdene Park.*

The diagrams show that there are two different ways in which the routes of the various persons involved in the Ravensdene

Mystery may be traced, without any path ever crossing another. It depends whether the butler, E, went to the north or the south of the gamekeeper's cottage, and the gamekeeper, A, went to the south or the north of the hall. But it will be found that the only persons who could have approached Mr. Cyril Hastings without

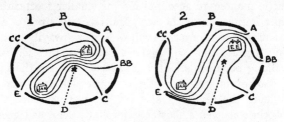

crossing a path were the butler, E, and the man, C. It was, however, a fact that the butler retired to bed five minutes before midnight, whereas Mr. Hastings did not leave his friend's house until midnight. Therefore the criminal must have been the man who entered the park at C.

66.—*The Buried Treasure.*

The field must have contained between 179 and 180 acres—to be more exact, 179.37254 acres. Had the measurements been 3, 2, and 4 furlongs respectively from successive corners, then the field would have been 209.70537 acres in area.

One method of solving this problem is as follows. Find the area of triangle APB in terms of x, the side of the square. Double the result $=xy$. Divide by x and then square, and we have the value of y^2 in terms of x. Similarly find value of z^2 in terms of x; then solve the equation $y^2+z^2=3^2$, which will come out in the form $x^4-20x^2=-37$. Therefore $x^2=10+\sqrt{63}=17.937254$ square furlongs, very nearly, and as there are ten acres in one square furlong, this equals 179.37254 acres. If we take the negative root of the equation, we get the area of the field as 20.62746 acres, in which case the treasure would have been buried outside the field, as in Diagram 2. But this solution is excluded by the condition that the treasure was buried in the field. The words

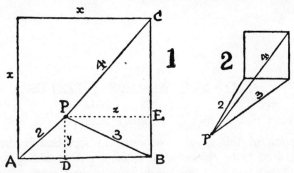

were, " The document . . . states clearly that the field is square, and that the treasure is buried in it."

THE PROFESSOR'S PUZZLES

67.—*The Coinage Puzzle.*

THE point of this puzzle turns on the fact that if the magic square were to be composed of whole numbers adding up 15 in all ways, the two must be placed in one of the corners. Otherwise fractions must be used, and these are supplied in the puzzle by the

4s. 6d.	4s. 4s.	2s.6d.
2s. 1s.	5s.	5s. 2s.
5s. 2s 6d.	2 s.	5s. 6d.

employment of sixpences and half-crowns. I give the arrangement requiring the fewest possible current English coins—fifteen. It will be seen that the amount in each corner is a fractional one, the sum required in the total being a whole number of shillings.

68.—*The Postage Stamps Puzzles.*

The first of these puzzles is based on a similar principle, though it is really much easier, because the condition that nine of the stamps must be of different values makes their selection a simple matter, though how they are to be placed requires a little thought

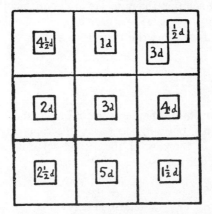

or trial until one knows the rule respecting putting the fractions in the corners. I give the solution.

I also show the solution to the second stamp puzzle. All the

columns, rows, and diagonals add up 1s. 6d. There is no stamp on one square, and the conditions did not forbid this omission. The stamps at present in circulation are these :—½d., 1d., 1½d., 2d., 2½d., 3d., 4d., 5d., 6d., 9d., 10d., 1s., 2s. 6d., 5s., 10s., £1, and £5.

In the first solution the numbers are in arithmetical progression —1, 1½, 2, 2½, 3, 3½, 4, 4½, 5. But any nine numbers will form a magic square if we can write them thus :—

$$1 \quad 2 \quad 3$$
$$7 \quad 8 \quad 9$$
$$13 \quad 14 \quad 15$$

where the horizontal differences are all alike and the vertical differences all alike, but not necessarily the same as the horizontal. This happens in the case of the second solution, the numbers of which may be written :—

$$0 \quad 1 \quad 2$$
$$5 \quad 6 \quad 7$$
$$10 \quad 11 \quad 12$$

Also in the case of the solution to No. 67, the Coinage Puzzle, the numbers are, in shillings :—

$$2 \quad 2\tfrac{1}{2} \quad 3$$
$$4\tfrac{1}{2} \quad 5 \quad 5\tfrac{1}{2}$$
$$7 \quad 7\tfrac{1}{2} \quad 8$$

If there are to be nine *different* numbers, o may occur once (as in the solution to No. 22). Yet one might construct squares with negative numbers, as follows :—

$$-2 \quad -1 \quad 0$$
$$5 \quad 6 \quad 7$$
$$12 \quad 13 \quad 14$$

69.—*The Frogs and Tumblers.*

It is perfectly true, as the Professor said, that there is only one solution (not counting a reversal) to this puzzle. The frogs that jump are George in the third horizontal row; Chang, the artful-looking batrachian at the end of the fourth row ; and Wilhelmina, the fair creature in the seventh row. George jumps downwards to the second tumbler in the seventh row; Chang, who can only leap short distances in consequence of chronic rheumatism, removes somewhat unwillingly to the glass just above him—the eighth in the third row; while Wilhelmina, with all the sprightliness of

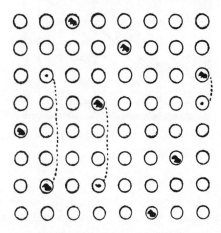

her youth and sex, performs the very creditable saltatory feat of leaping to the fourth tumbler in the fourth row. In their new positions, as shown in the accompanying diagram, it will be found that of the eight frogs no two are in line vertically, horizontally, or diagonally.

70.—*Romeo and Juliet.*

This is rather a difficult puzzle, though, as the Professor remarked when Hawkhurst hit on the solution, it is "just one of those puzzles that a person might solve at a glance" by pure luck. Yet when the solution, with its pretty, symmetrical arrangement, is seen, it looks ridiculously simple.

It will be found that Romeo reaches Juliet's balcony after visiting every house once and only once, and making fourteen turnings, not counting the turn he makes at starting. These are

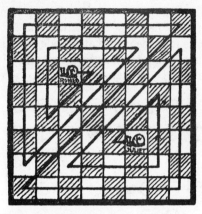

the fewest turnings possible, and the problem can only be solved
by the route shown or its reversal.

71.—Romeo's Second Journey.

In order to take his trip through all the white squares only
with the fewest possible turnings, Romeo would do well to adopt

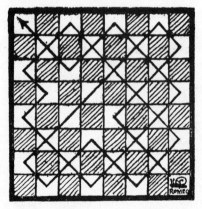

the route I have shown, by means of which only sixteen turnings
are required to perform the feat. The Professor informs me that

the Helix Aspersa, or common or garden snail, has a peculiar aversion to making turnings—so much so that one specimen with which he made experiments went off in a straight line one night and has never come back since.

72.—*The Frogs who would a-wooing go.*

This is one of those puzzles in which a plurality of solutions is practically unavoidable. There are two or three positions into which four frogs may jump so as to form five rows with four

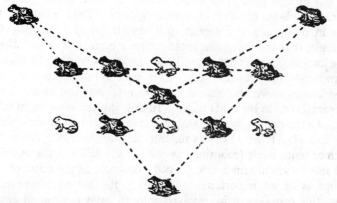

in each row, but the case I have given is the most satisfactory arrangement.

The frogs that have jumped have left their astral bodies behind, in order to show the reader the positions which they originally occupied. Chang, the frog in the middle of the upper row, suffering from rheumatism, as explained above in the Frogs and Tumblers solution, makes the shortest jump of all—a little distance between the two rows ; George and Wilhelmina leap from the ends of the lower row to some distance N. by N.W. and N. by N.E. respectively ; while the frog in the middle of the lower row, whose name the Professor forgot to state, goes direct S.

MISCELLANEOUS PUZZLES

73.—*The Game of Kayles.*

To win at this game you must, sooner or later, leave your opponent an even number of similar groups. Then whatever he does in one group you repeat in a similar group. Suppose, for example, that you leave him these groups : o . o . ooo . ooo. Now, if he knocks down a single, you knock down a single ; if he knocks down two in one triplet, you knock down two in the other triplet ; if he knocks down the central kayle in a triplet, you knock down the central one in the other triplet. In this way you must eventually win. As the game is started with the arrangement o . ooooooooooo, the first player can always win, but only by knocking down the sixth or tenth kayle (counting the one already fallen as the second), and this leaves in either case o . ooo . ooooooo, as the order of the groups is of no importance. Whatever the second player now does, this can always be resolved into an even number of equal groups. Let us suppose that he knocks down the single one; then we play to leave him oo . ooooooo. Now, whatever he does we can afterwards leave him either ooo . ooo or o . oo . ooo. We know why the former wins, and the latter wins also; because, however he may play, we can always leave him either o . o, or o . o . o . o, or oo . oo, as the case may be. The complete analysis I can now leave for the amusement of the reader.

74.—*The Broken Chessboard.*

The illustration will show how the thirteen pieces can be put together so as to construct the perfect board, and the reverse prob-

lem of cutting these particular pieces out will be found equally entertaining.

Compare with Nos. 293 and 294 in *A. in M.*

75.—*The Spider and the Fly.*

Though this problem was much discussed in the *Daily Mail* from 18th January to 7th February 1905, when it appeared to create great public interest, it was actually first propounded by me in the *Weekly Dispatch* of 14th June 1903.

Imagine the room to be a cardboard box. Then the box may be cut in various different ways, so that the cardboard may be laid flat on the table. I show four of these ways, and indicate in every case the relative positions of the spider and the fly, and the straightened course which the spider must take without going off the cardboard. These are the four most favourable cases, and it will be found that the shortest route is in No. 4, for it is only 40 feet in length (add the square of 32 to the square of 24 and extract the square root). It will be seen that the spider actually passes along five of the six sides of the room! Having marked the route, fold the box up (removing the side the spider does not use), and the appearance of the shortest course is rather surprising. If the spider had taken what most persons will consider obviously the shortest route (that shown in No. 1), he would have gone 42 feet ! Route No. 2 is 43.174 feet in length, and Route No. 3 is 40.718 feet.

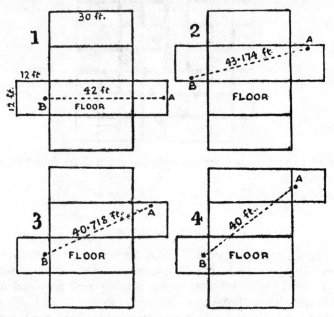

I will leave the reader to discover which are the shortest routes when the spider and the fly are 2, 3, 4, 5, and 6 feet from the ceiling and the floor respectively.

76.—*The Perplexed Cellarman.*

Brother John gave the first man three large bottles and one small bottleful of wine, and one large and three small empty bottles. To each of the other two men he gave two large and three small bottles of wine, and two large and one small empty bottle. Each of the three then receives the same quantity of wine, and the same number of each size of bottle.

77.—*Making a Flag.*

The diagram shows how the piece of bunting is to be cut into two pieces. Lower the piece on the right one " tooth," and they will form a perfect square, with the roses symmetrically placed.

It will be found interesting to compare this with No. 154 in *A. in M.*

78.—*Catching the Hogs.*

A very short examination of this puzzle game should convince the reader that Hendrick can never catch the black hog, and that the white hog can never be caught by Katrün.

Each hog merely runs in and out of one of the nearest corners and can never be captured. The fact is, curious as it must at first sight appear, a Dutchman cannot catch a black hog, and a Dutchwoman can never capture a white one! But each can, without difficulty, catch one of the other colour.

So if the first player just determines that he will send Hendrick after the white porker and Katrün after the black one, he will have no difficulty whatever in securing both in a very few moves.

It is, in fact, so easy that there is no necessity whatever to give the line of play. We thus, by means of the game, solve the puzzle in real life, why the Dutchman and his wife could not catch their pigs : in their simplicity and ignorance of the peculiarities of Dutch hogs, each went after the wrong animal.

The little principle involved in this puzzle is that known to chess-players as " getting the opposition." The rule, in the case of my puzzle (where the moves resemble rook moves in chess, with the added condition that the rook may only move to an adjoining square), is simply this. Where the number of squares on the same row, between the man or woman and the hog, is odd, the hog can never be captured ; where the number of squares is even, a capture is possible. The number of squares between Hendrick and the black hog, and between Katrün and the white hog, is 1 (an odd number), therefore these individuals cannot catch the animals they are facing. But the number between Hendrick and the white hog, and between Katrün and the black one, is 6 (an even number), therefore they may easily capture those behind them.

79.—*The Thirty-one Game.*

By leading with a 5 the first player can always win. If your opponent plays another 5, you play a 2 and score 12. Then as often as he plays a 5 you play a 2, and if at any stage he drops out of the series, 3, 10, 17, 24, 31, you step in and win. If after your lead of 5 he plays anything but another 5, you make 10 or 17 and win. The first player may also win by leading a 1 or a 2, but the play is complicated. It is, however, well worth the reader's study.

80.—*The Chinese Railways.*

This puzzle was artfully devised by the yellow man. It is not a matter for wonder that the representatives of the five countries interested were bewildered. It would have puzzled the engineers a good deal to construct those circuitous routes so that the various trains might run with safety. Diagram 1 shows directions for the five systems of lines, so that no line shall ever cross another, and this appears to be the method that would require the shortest possible mileage.

The reader may wish to know how many different solutions there are to the puzzle. To this I should answer that the number is indeterminate, and I will explain why. If we simply consider the case of line A alone, then one route would be Diagram 2, another 3, another 4, and another 5. If 3 is different from 2, as it undoubtedly is, then we must regard 5 as different from 4. But a

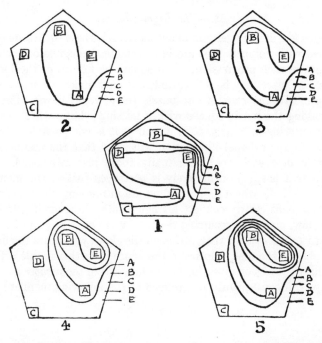

glance at the four diagrams, 2, 3, 4, 5, in succession will show that we may continue this " winding up " process for ever ; and as there will always be an unobstructed way (however long and circuitous) from stations B and E to their respective main lines, it is evident that the number of routes for line A alone is infinite. Therefore the number of complete solutions must also be infinite, if railway lines, like other lines, have no breadth ; and indeterminate, unless we are told the greatest number of parallel lines that it is possible to construct in certain places. If some clear condition, restricting these " windings up," were given, there would be no great difficulty in giving the number of solutions. With any reasonable limitation of the kind, the number would, I calculate, be little short of two thousand, surprising though it may appear.

81.—*The Eight Clowns.*

This is a little novelty in magic squares. These squares may be formed with numbers that are in arithmetical progression, or that are not in such progression. If a square be formed of the former class, one place may be left vacant, but only under particular conditions. In the case of our puzzle there would be no difficulty in making the magic square with 9 missing ; but with 1 missing (that is, using 2, 3, 4, 5, 6, 7, 8, and 9) it is not possible. But a glance at the original illustration will show that the numbers we have to deal with are not actually those just mentioned. The clown that has a 9 on his body is portrayed just at the moment when two balls which he is juggling are in mid-air. The positions of these balls clearly convert his figure into the recurring decimal .9. Now, since the recurring decimal .9 is equal to $\frac{9}{9}$, and therefore to 1, it is evident that, although the clown who bears the figure 1 is absent, the man who bears the figure 9 by this simple artifice has for the occasion given his *figure* the value of the *number* 1. The troupe can consequently be grouped in the following manner :—

$$
\begin{array}{ccc}
7 & & 5 \\
2 & 4 & 6 \\
3 & 8 & .\dot{9}
\end{array}
$$

Every column, every row, and each of the two diagonals now add up to 12. This is the correct solution to the puzzle.

82.—*The Wizard's Arithmetic.*

This puzzle is both easy and difficult, for it is a very simple matter to find one of the multipliers, which is 86. If we multiply

8 by 86, all we need do is to place the 6 in front and the 8 behind
in order to get the correct answer, 688. But the second number
is not to be found by mere trial. It is 71, and the number to be
multiplied is no less than 16393442622950819672131147540983-
6065573770491803272787. If you want to multiply this by 71, all
you have to do is to place another 1 at the beginning and another
7 at the end—a considerable saving of labour! These two, and
the example shown by the wizard, are the only two-figure multipliers, but the number to be multiplied may always be increased.
Thus, if you prefix to 41096 the number 41095890, repeated any
number of times, the result may always be multiplied by 83 in the
wizard's peculiar manner.

If we add the figures of any number together and then, if necessary, again add, we at last get a single-figure number. This I call
the " digital root." Thus, the digital root of 521 is 8, and of 697
it is 4. This digital analysis is extensively dealt with in *A. in M.*
Now, it is evident that the digital roots of the two numbers
required by the puzzle must produce the same root in sum and
product. This can only happen when the roots of the two numbers
are 2 and 2, or 9 and 9, or 3 and 6, or 5 and 8. Therefore the two-
figure multiplier must have a digital root of 2, 3, 5, 6, 8, or 9. There
are ten such numbers in each case. I write out all the sixty, then
I strike out all those numbers where the second figure is higher
than the first, and where the two figures are alike (thirty-six numbers
in all) ; also all remaining numbers where the first figure is odd
and the second figure even (seven numbers) ; also all multiples
of 5 (three more numbers). The numbers 21 and 62 I reject on
inspection, for reasons that I will not enter into. I then have left,
out of the original sixty, only the following twelve numbers :
83, 63, 81, 84, 93, 42, 51, 87, 41, 86, 53, and 71. These are the only
possible multipliers that I have really to examine.

My process is now as curious as it is simple in working. First
trying 83, I deduct 10 and call it 73. Adding 0's to the second
figure, I say if 30000, etc., ever has a remainder 43 when divided
by 73, the dividend will be the required multiplier for 83. I get

the 43 in this way. The only multiplier of 3 that produces an 8 in the digits place is 6. I therefore multiply 73 by 6 and get 438, or 43 after rejecting the 8. Now, 300,000 divided by 73 leaves the remainder 43, and the dividend is 4,109. To this I add the 6 mentioned above and get 41,096 × 83, the example given on page 129.

In trying the even numbers there are two cases to be considered. Thus, taking 86, we may say that if 60000, etc., when divided by 76 leaves either 22 or 60 (because 3 × 6 and 8 × 6 both produce 8), we get a solution. But I reject the former on inspection, and see that 60 divided by 76 is 0, leaving a remainder 60. Therefore 8 × 86 = 688, the other example. It will be found in the case of 71 that 100000, etc., divided by 61 gives a remainder 42, (7 × 61 = 427) after producing the long dividend at the beginning of this article, with the 7 added.

The other multipliers fail to produce a solution, so 83, 86, and 71 are the only three possible multipliers. Those who are familiar with the principle of recurring decimals (as somewhat explained in my next note on No. 83, "The Ribbon Problem") will understand the conditions under which the remainders repeat themselves after certain periods, and will only find it necessary in two or three cases to make any lengthy divisions. It clearly follows that there is an unlimited number of multiplicands for each multiplier.

83.—*The Ribbon Problem.*

The solution is as follows : Place this rather lengthy number on the ribbon, 0212765957446808510638297872340425531914893617. It may be multiplied by any number up to 46 inclusive to give the same order of figures in the ring. The number previously given can be multiplied by any number up to 16. I made the limit 9 in order to put readers off the scent. The fact is these two numbers are simply the recurring decimals that equal $\frac{1}{47}$ and $\frac{1}{47}$ respectively. Multiply the one by seventeen and the other by forty-seven, and you will get all nines in each case.

In transforming a vulgar fraction, say $\frac{1}{17}$, to a decimal

fraction, we proceed as below, adding as many noughts to the
dividend as we like until there is no remainder, or until we get
a recurring series of figures, or until we have carried it as far as
we require, since every additional figure in a never-ending decimal
carries us nearer and nearer to exactitude.

```
17) 100 (.058823
    85
    ───
    150
    136
    ───
    140
    136
    ───
     40
     34
    ───
     60
     51
    ───
      9
```

Now, since all powers of 10 can only contain factors of the
powers of 2 and 5, it clearly follows that your decimal never will
come to an end if any other factor than these occurs in the de-
nominator of your vulgar fraction. Thus, $\frac{1}{2}$, $\frac{1}{4}$, and $\frac{1}{8}$ give us the
exact decimals, .5, .25, and .125; $\frac{1}{5}$ and $\frac{1}{25}$ give us .2 and .04;
$\frac{1}{10}$ and $\frac{1}{20}$ give us .1 and .05: because the denominators are all
composed of 2 and 5 factors. But if you wish to convert $\frac{1}{3}$, $\frac{1}{6}$,
or $\frac{1}{7}$, your division sum will never end, but you will get these
decimals, .33333, etc., .166666, etc., and .142857142857142857,
etc., where, in the first case, the 3 keeps on repeating for ever
and ever; in the second case the 6 is the repeater, and in the
last case we get the recurring period of 142857. In the case of
$\frac{1}{17}$ (in "The Ribbon Problem") we find the circulating period
to be .0588235294117647.

Now, in the division sum above, the successive remainders are

1, 10, 15, 14, 4, 6, 9, etc., and these numbers I have inserted around the inner ring of the diagram. It will be seen that every number from 1 to 16 occurs once, and that if we multiply our ribbon number by any one of the numbers in the inner ring its position indicates exactly the point at which the product will begin. Thus, if we multiply by 4, the product will be 235, etc. ; if we multiply by 6,

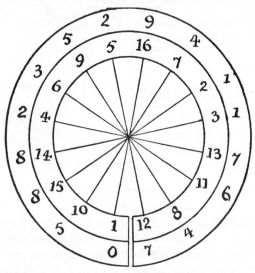

352, etc. We can therefore multiply by any number from 1 to 16 and get the desired result.

The kernel of the puzzle is this: Any prime number, with the exception of 2 and 5, which are the factors of 10, will exactly divide without remainder a number consisting of as many nines as the number itself, less one. Thus 999999 (six 9's) is divisible by 7, sixteen 9's are divisible by 17, eighteen 9's by 19, and so on. This is always the case, though frequently fewer 9's will suffice; for one 9 is divisible by 3, two by 11, six by 13, when our ribbon rule for consecutive multipliers breaks down and another law comes in. Therefore, since the 0 and 7 at the ends of the ribbon may not be removed, we must seek a fraction with a prime denominator ending in 7 that gives a full period circulator. We try 37, and find that it gives a short period decimal, .027, because 37 exactly divides 999; it, therefore, will not do. We next examine 47, and find that it gives us the full period circulator, in 46 figures, at the beginning of this article.

If you cut any of these full period circulators in half and place one half under the other, you will find that they will add up all 9's; so you need only work out one half and then write down the complements. Thus, in the ribbon above, if you add 05882352 to 94117647 the result is 99999999, and so with our long solution number. Note also in the diagram above that not only are the opposite numbers on the outer ring complementary, always making 9 when added, but that opposite numbers in the inner ring, our remainders, are also complementary, adding to 17 in every case. I ought perhaps to point out that in limiting our multipliers to the first nine numbers it seems just possible that a short period circulator might give a solution in fewer figures, but there are reasons for thinking it improbable.

84.—*The Japanese Ladies and the Carpet.*

If the squares had not to be all the same size, the carpet could be cut in four pieces in any one of the three manners shown. In each case the two pieces marked A will fit together and form one of the three squares, the other two squares being entire. But in order to have the squares exactly equal in size, we shall require six pieces, as shown in the larger diagram. No. 1 is a complete square, pieces 4 and 5 will form a second square, and pieces 2, 3, and 6 will form the third—all of exactly the same size.

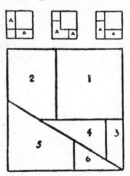

If with the three equal squares we form the rectangle IDBA, then the mean proportional of the two sides of the rectangle will be the side of a square of equal area. Produce AB to C, making

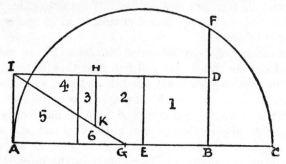

BC equal to BD. Then place the point of the compasses at E (midway between A and C) and describe the arc AC. I am showing the quite general method for converting rectangles to squares, but in this particular case we may, of course, at once place our compasses at E, which requires no finding. Produce the line BD, cutting the arc in F, and BF will be the required side of the square. Now mark off AG and DH, each equal to BF, and make the cut IG, and also the cut HK from H, perpendicular to ID. The six pieces produced are numbered as in the diagram on last page.

It will be seen that I have here given the reverse method first : to cut the three small squares into six pieces to form a large square. In the case of our puzzle we can proceed as follows :—

Make LM equal to half the diagonal ON. Draw the line NM and drop from L a perpendicular on NM. Then LP will be the side of all the three squares of combined area equal to the large square QNLO. The reader can now cut out without difficulty the six pieces, as shown in the numbered square on the last page.

85.—*Captain Longbow and the Bears.*

It might have struck the reader that the story of the bear impaled on the North Pole had no connection with the problem that followed. As a matter of fact it is essential to a solution. Eleven bears cannot possibly be arranged to form of themselves seven rows of bears with four bears in every row. But it is a different matter when Captain Longbow informs us that "they

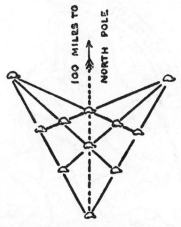

had so placed themselves that *there were*" seven rows of four bears. For if they were grouped as shown in the diagram, so that three of the bears, as indicated, were in line with the North Pole, that impaled animal would complete the seventh row of four, which cannot be obtained in any other way. It obviously does not affect the problem whether this seventh row is a hundred miles long or a hundred feet, so long as they were really in a straight line—a point that might perhaps be settled by the captain's pocket compass.

86.—*The English Tour.*

It was required to show how a resident at the town marked A might visit every one of the towns once, and only once, and finish up his tour at Z. This puzzle conceals a little trick. After the solver has demonstrated to his satisfaction that it cannot be done in accordance with the conditions as he at first understood them, he should carefully examine the wording in order to find some flaw. It was said, " This would be easy enough if he were able to cut across country by road, as well as by rail, but he is not."

Now, although he is prohibited from cutting across country by road, nothing is said about his going by sea! If, therefore, we carefully look again at the map, we shall find that two towns, and two only, lie on the sea coast. When he reaches one of these towns he takes his departure on board a coasting vessel and sails to the other port. The annexed illustration shows, by a dark line, the complete route.

This problem should be compared with No. 250, " The Grand Tour," in *A. in M.* It can be simplified in practically an identical manner, but as there is here no choice on the first stage from A, the solutions are necessarily quite different. See also solution to No. 94.

87.—*The Chifu-Chemulpo Puzzle.*

The solution is as follows. You may accept the invitation to " try to do it in twenty moves," but you will never succeed in performing the feat. The fewest possible moves are twenty-six. Play the cars so as to reach the following positions :—

$$\frac{\text{E}5678}{1234} = \text{10 moves.}$$

$$\frac{\text{E}56}{123\quad 87\quad 4} = \text{2 moves.}$$

$$\frac{56}{\text{E}312\quad 87\quad 4} = \text{5 moves.}$$

$$\frac{\text{E}}{87654321} = \text{9 moves.}$$

Twenty-six moves in all.

88.—*The Eccentric Market-woman.*

The smallest possible number of eggs that Mrs. Covey could have taken to market is 719. After selling half the number and giving half an egg over she would have 359 left ; after the second transaction she would have 239 left ; after the third deal, 179 ; and after the fourth, 143. This last number she could divide equally among her thirteen friends, giving each 11, and she would not have broken an egg.

89.—*The Primrose Puzzle.*

The two words that solve this puzzle are BLUEBELL and PEARTREE. Place the letters as follows : B 3—1, L 6—8, U 5—3, E 4—6, B 7—5, E 2—4, L 9—7, L 9—2. This means that you take B, jump from 3 to 1, and write it down on 1 ; and so on. The second word can be inserted in the same order. The solution depends on finding those words in which the second and eighth letters are the same, and also the fourth and sixth the same, because these letters interchange without destroying the words. MARITIMA (or sea-pink) would also solve the puzzle if it were an English word.

Compare with No. 226 in *A. in M.*

90.—*The Round Table.*

Here is the way of arranging the seven men :—

A	B	C	D	E	F	G
A	C	D	B	G	E	F
A	D	B	C	F	G	E
A	G	B	F	E	C	D
A	F	C	E	G	D	B
A	E	D	G	F	B	C
A	C	E	B	G	F	D
A	D	G	C	F	E	B
A	B	F	D	E	G	C
A	E	F	D	C	G	B
A	G	E	B	D	F	C
A	F	G	C	B	E	D
A	E	B	F	C	D	G
A	G	C	E	D	B	F
A	F	D	G	B	C	E

Of course, at a circular table, A will be next to the man at the end of the line.

I first gave this problem for six persons on ten days, in the *Daily Mail* for the 13th and 16th October 1905, and it has since been discussed in various periodicals by mathematicians. Of course, it is easily seen that the maximum number of sittings for n persons is $\frac{(n-1)(n-2)}{2}$ ways. The comparatively easy method for solving all cases where *n* is a prime + 1 was first discovered by Ernest Bergholt. I then pointed out the form and construction of a solution that I had obtained for 10 persons, from which E. D. Bewley found a general method for all even numbers. The odd numbers, however, are extremely difficult, and for a long time no progress could be made with their solution, the only numbers that could be worked being 7 (given above) and 5, 9, 17, and 33, these last four being all powers of 2 + 1. At last, however (though not without much difficulty), I discovered a subtle method for solving all cases, and have written out schedules for every number up to 25 inclusive. The case of 11 has been solved also by W. Nash. Perhaps the reader will like to try his hand at 13. He will find it an extraordinarily hard nut.

The solutions for all cases up to 12 inclusive are given in *A. in M.*, pp. 205, 206.

91.—*The Five Tea Tins.*

There are twelve ways of arranging the boxes without considering the pictures. If the thirty pictures were all different the answer would be 93,312. But the necessary deductions for cases where changes of boxes may be made without affecting the order of pictures amount to 1,728, and the boxes may therefore be arranged, in accordance with the conditions, in 91,584 different ways. I will leave my readers to discover for themselves how the figures are to be arrived at.

92.—*The Four Porkers.*

The number of ways in which the four pigs may be placed in the thirty-six sties in accordance with the conditions is seventeen, including the example that I gave, not counting the reversals and reflections of these arrangements as different. Jaenisch, in his *Analyse Mathématique au jeu des Échecs* (1862), quotes the statement that there are just twenty-one solutions to the little problem on which this puzzle is based. As I had myself only recorded seventeen, I examined the matter again, and found that he was in error, and, doubtless, had mistaken reversals for different arrangements.

Here are the seventeen answers. The figures indicate the rows, and their positions show the columns. Thus, 104603 means that we place a pig in the first row of the *first* column, in no row of the *second* column, in the fourth row of the *third* column, in the sixth row of the *fourth* column, in no row of the *fifth* column, and in the third row of the *sixth* column. The arrangement E is that which I gave in diagram form :—

A. 104603	J. 206104
B. 136002	K. 241005
C. 140502	L. 250014
D. 140520	M. 250630
E. 160025	N. 260015
F. 160304	O. 261005
G. 201405	P. 261040
H. 201605	Q. 306104
I. 205104	—

It will be found that forms N and Q are semi-symmetrical with regard to the centre, and therefore give only two arrangements each by reversal and reflection ; that form H is quarter-symmetrical, and gives only four arrangements ; while all the fourteen others yield by reversal and reflection eight arrangements each. Therefore the pigs may be placed in $(2 \times 2) + (4 \times 1) + (8 \times 14) = 120$ different ways by reversing and reflecting all the seventeen forms.

Three pigs alone may be placed so that every sty is in line with a pig, provided that the pigs are not forbidden to be in line with one another ; but there is only one way of doing it (if we do not count reversals as different), as follows : 105030.

93.—*The Number Blocks.*

Arrange the blocks so as to form the two multiplication sums 915×64 and 732×80, and the product in both cases will be the same : 58,560.

94.—*Foxes and Geese.*

The smallest possible number of moves is twenty-two—that is, eleven for the foxes and eleven for the geese. Here is one way of solving the puzzle :

10—5	11—6	12—7	5—12	6—1	7—6
1—8	2—9	3—4	8—3	9—10	4—9

12—7	1—8	6—1	7—2	8—3
3—4	10—5	9—10	4—11	5—12

Of course, the reader will play the first move in the top line, then the first move in the second line, then the second move in the top line, and so on alternately.

In *A. in M.*, p. 230, I have explained fully my " buttons and string " method of solving puzzles on chequered boards. In Diagram A is shown the puzzle in the form in which it may be pre-

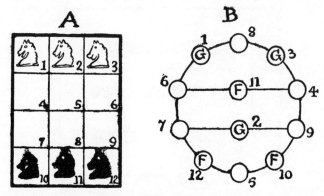

sented on a portion of the chessboard with six knights. A comparison with the illustration on page 141 will show that I have there dispensed with the necessity of explaining the knight's move to the uninstructed reader by lines that indicate those moves. The two puzzles are the same thing in different dress. Now compare page 141 with Diagram B, and it will be seen that by disentangling the strings I have obtained a simplified diagram without altering the essential relations between the buttons or discs. The reader will now satisfy himself without any difficulty that the puzzle requires eleven moves for the foxes and eleven for the geese. He will see that a goose on 1 or 3 must go to 8, to avoid being one move from a fox and to enable the fox on 11 to come on to the ring. If we play 1—8, then it is clearly best to play 10—5 and not 12—5 for the foxes. When they are all on the circle, then they simply promenade round it in a clockwise direction, taking care to reserve 8—3 and 5—12 for the final moves. It is thus rendered ridiculously easy by this method. See also notes on solutions to Nos. 13 and 85.

95.—*Robinson Crusoe's Table.*

The diagram shows how the piece of wood should be cut in two pieces to form the square table-top. A, B, C, D are the corners of

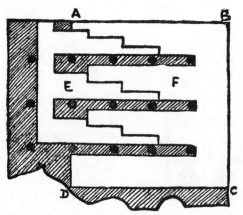

the table. The way in which the piece E fits into the piece F will be obvious to the eye of the reader. The shaded part is the wood that is discarded.

96.—*The Fifteen Orchards.*

The number must be the least common multiple of 1, 2, 3, etc., up to 15, that, when divided by 7, leaves the remainder 1, by 9 leaves 3, by 11 leaves 10, by 13 leaves 3, and by 14 leaves 8. Such a number is 120. The next number is 360,480, but as we have no record of a tree—especially a very young one—bearing anything like such a large number of apples, we may take 120 to be the only answer that is acceptable.

97.—*The Perplexed Plumber.*

The rectangular closed cistern that shall hold a given quantity of water and yet have the smallest possible surface of metal must be a perfect cube—that is, a cistern every side of which is a square. For 1,000 cubic feet of water the internal dimensions will be 10 ft. × 10 ft. × 10 ft., and the zinc required will be 600 square feet. In the case of a cistern without a top the proportions will be exactly half a cube. These are the " exact proportions " asked for in the second case. The exact dimensions cannot be given, but 12.6 ft. × 12.6 ft. × 6.3 ft. is a close approximation. The cistern will hold a little too much water, at which the buyer will not complain, and it will involve the plumber in a trifling loss not worth considering.

98.—*The Nelson Column.*

If you take a sheet of paper and mark it with a diagonal line, as in Figure A, you will find that when you roll it into cylindrical form, with the line outside, it will appear as in Figure B.

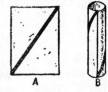

It will be seen that the spiral (in one complete turn) is merely the hypotenuse of a right-angled triangle, of which the length and width of the paper are the other two sides. In the puzzle given, the lengths of the two sides of the triangle are 40 ft. (one-fifth of 200 ft.) and 16 ft. 8 in. Therefore the hypotenuse is 43 ft. 4 in. The length of the garland is therefore five times as long—216 ft. 8 in. A curious feature of the puzzle is the fact that with the dimensions given the result is exactly the sum of the height and the circumference.

99.—*The Two Errand Boys.*

All that is necessary is to add the two distances at which they meet to twice their difference. Thus 720 + 400 + 640 = 1760 yards, or one mile, which is the distance required. Or, put another way, three times the first distance less the second distance will always give the answer, only the first distance should be more than two-thirds of the second.

100.—*On the Ramsgate Sands.*

Just six different rings may be formed without breaking the conditions. Here is one way of effecting the arrangements.

A	B	C	D	E	F	G	H	I	J	K	L	M
A	C	E	G	I	K	M	B	D	F	H	J	L
A	D	G	J	M	C	F	I	L	B	E	H	K
A	E	I	M	D	H	L	C	G	K	B	F	J
A	F	K	C	H	M	E	J	B	G	L	D	I
A	G	M	F	L	E	K	D	J	C	I	B	H

Join the ends and you have the six rings.

Lucas devised a simple mechanical method for obtaining the *n* rings that may be formed under the conditions by $2n + 1$ children.

101.—*The Three Motor-Cars.*

The only set of three numbers, of two, three, and five figures respectively, that will fulfil the required conditions is 27 × 594 = 16,038. These three numbers contain all the nine digits and 0, without repetition ; the first two numbers multiplied together make the third, and the second is exactly twenty-two times the first. If the numbers might contain one, four, and five figures respectively, there would be many correct answers, such as $3 \times 5,694 = 17,082$; but it is a curious fact that there is only one answer to the problem as propounded, though it is no easy matter to prove that this is the case.

102.—*A Reversible Magic Square.*

It will be seen that in the arrangement given every number is different, and all the columns, all the rows, and each of the two

diagonals, add up 179, whether you turn the page upside down or not. The reader will notice that I have not used the figures 3, 4, 5, 8, or 0.

103.—*The Tube Railway.*

There are 640 different routes. A general formula for puzzles of this kind is not practicable. We have obviously only to consider the variations of route between B and E. Here there are nine sections or " lines," but it is impossible for a train, under the conditions, to traverse more than seven of these lines in any route. In the following table by " directions " is meant the order of stations irrespective of "routes." Thus, the "direction" BCDE gives nine "routes," because there are three ways of getting from B to C, and three ways of getting from D to E. But the "direction" BDCE admits of no variation ; therefore yields only one route.

2 two-line directions of	3 routes	—	6
1 three-line	,,	,,	1	,,	—	1
1 ,,	,,	,,	9	,,	—	9
2 four-line	,,	,,	6	,,	—	12
2 ,,	,,	,,	18	,,	—	36
6 five-line	,,	,,	6	,,	—	36
2 ,,	,,	,,	18	,,	—	36
2 six-line	,,	,,	36	,,	—	72
12 seven-line	,,	,,	36	,,	—	432

Total 640

We thus see that there are just 640 different routes in all, which is the correct answer to the puzzle.

104.—*The Skipper and the Sea-Serpent.*

Each of the three pieces was clearly three cables long. But Simon persisted in assuming that the cuts were made transversely, or across, and that therefore the complete length was nine cables. The skipper, however, explained (and the point is quite as veracious as the rest of his yarn) that his cuts were made longitudinally— straight from the tip of the nose to the tip of the tail ! The complete length was therefore only three cables, the same as each piece. Simon was not asked the exact length of the serpent, but how long it *must* have been. It must have been at least three cables long, though it might have been (the skipper's statement apart) anything from that up to nine cables, according to the direction of the cuts.

105.—*The Dorcas Society.*

If there were twelve ladies in all, there would be 132 kisses among the ladies alone, leaving twelve more to be exchanged with the curate—six to be given by him and six to be received. Therefore, of the twelve ladies, six would be his sisters. Consequently, if twelve could do the work in four and a half months, six ladies would do it in twice the time—four and a half months longer—which is the correct answer.

At first sight there might appear to be some ambiguity about the words, " Everybody kissed everybody else, except, of course, the bashful young man himself." Might this not be held to imply that all the ladies immodestly kissed the curate, although they were not (except the sisters) kissed by him in return ? No ; be- cause, in that case, it would be found that there must have been twelve girls, not one of whom was a sister, which is contrary to the conditions. If, again, it should be held that the sisters might not, according to the wording, have kissed their brother, although he kissed them, I reply that in that case there must have been twelve girls, all of whom must have been his sisters. And the reference to the ladies who might have worked exclusively of the sisters shuts out the possibility of this.

106.—*The Adventurous Snail.*

At the end of seventeen days the snail will have climbed 17 ft., and at the end of its eighteenth day-time task it will be at the top. It instantly begins slipping while sleeping, and will be 2 ft. down the other side at the end of the eighteenth day of twenty-four hours. How long will it take over the remaining 18 ft. ? If it slips 2 ft. at night it clearly overcomes the tendency to slip 2 ft. during the daytime, in climbing up. In rowing up a river we have the stream against us, but in coming down it is with us and helps us. If the snail can climb 3 ft. and overcome the tendency to slip 2 ft. in twelve hours' ascent, it could with the same exertion crawl 5 ft. a day on the level. Therefore, in going down, the same exertion carries it 7 ft. in twelve hours—that is, 5 ft. by personal exertion and 2 ft. by slip. This, with the night slip, gives it a descending progress of 9 ft. in the twenty-four hours. It can, therefore, do the remaining 18 ft. in exactly two days, and the whole journey, up and down, will take it exactly twenty days.

107.—*The Four Princes.*

When Montucla, in his edition of Ozanam's *Recreations in Mathematics,* declared that " No more than three right-angled triangles, equal to each other, can be found in whole numbers, but we may find as many as we choose in fractions," he curiously overlooked the obvious fact that if you give all your sides a common denominator and then cancel that denominator you have the required answer in integers !

Every reader should know that if we take any two numbers, m and n, then $m^2 + n^2$, $m^2 - n^2$, and $2mn$ will be the three sides of a rational right-angled triangle. Here m and n are called generating numbers. To form three such triangles of equal area, we use the following simple formula, where m is the greater number :—

$$mn + m^2 + n^2 = a$$
$$m^2 - n^2 = b$$
$$2mn + n^2 = c$$

Now, if we form three triangles from the following pairs of generators, a and b, a and c, a and $b + c$, they will all be of equal area. This is the little problem respecting which Lewis Carroll says in his diary (see his *Life and Letters* by Collingwood, p. 343), " Sat up last night till 4 a.m., over a tempting problem, sent me from New York, ' to find three equal rational-sided right-angled triangles.' I found two . . . but could not find three ! "

The following is a subtle formula by means of which we may always find a R.A.T. equal in area to any given R.A.T. Let $z =$ hypotenuse, $b =$ base, $h =$ height, $a =$ area of the given triangle; then all we have to do is to form a R.A.T. from the generators z^2 and $4a$, and give each side the denominator $2z(b^2 - h^2)$, and we get the required answer in fractions. If we multiply all three sides of the original triangle by the denominator, we shall get at once a solution in whole numbers.

The answer to our puzzle in smallest possible numbers is as follows :-

First Prince . . .	518	1320	1418
Second Prince . . .	280	2442	2458
Third Prince . . .	231	2960	2969
Fourth Prince . . .	111	6160	6161

The area in every case is 341,880 square furlongs. I must here refrain from showing fully how I get these figures. I will explain, however, that the first three triangles are obtained, in the manner shown, from the numbers 3 and 4, which give the generators 37, 7 ; 37, 33 ; 37, 40. These three pairs of numbers solve the indeterminate equation, $a^3b - b^3a = 341,880$. If we can find another pair of values, the thing is done. These values are 56, 55, which generators give the last triangle. The next best answer that I have found is derived from 5 and 6, which give the generators 91, 11 ; 91, 85 ; 91, 96. The fourth pair of values is 63, 42.

The reader will understand from what I have written above that there is no limit to the number of rational-sided R.A.T.'s of equal area that may be found in whole numbers.

108.—*Plato and the Nines.*

The following is the simple solution of the three nines puzzle :—

$$\frac{9 + 9}{.9}$$

To divide 18 by .9 (or nine-tenths) we, of course, multiply by 10 and divide by 9. The result is 20, as required.

109.—*Noughts and Crosses.*

The solution is as follows : Between two players who thoroughly understand the play every game should be drawn. Neither player could ever win except through the blundering of his opponent. If Nought (the first player) takes the centre, Cross must take a corner, or Nought may beat him with certainty. If Nought takes a corner on his first play, Cross must take the centre at once, or again be beaten with certainty. If Nought leads with a side, both players must be very careful to prevent a loss, as there are numerous pit-falls. But Nought may safely lead anything and secure a draw, and he can only win through Cross's blunders.

110.—*Ovid's Game.*

The solution here is : The first player can always win, provided he plays to the centre on his first move. But a good variation of the game is to bar the centre for the first move of the first player. In that case the second player should take the centre at once. This should always end in a draw, but to ensure it the first player must play to two adjoining corners (such as 1 and 3) on his first and second moves. The game then requires great care on both sides.

111.—*The Farmer's Oxen.*

Sir Isaac Newton has shown us, in his *Universal Arithmetic*, that we may divide the bullocks in each case in two parts—one part to eat the increase, and the other the accumulated grass. The first will vary directly as the size of the field, and will not depend on the time ; the second part will also vary directly as the size of the field, and in addition inversely with the time. We find from the farmer's statements that 6 bullocks keep down the growth in a 10-acre field, and 6 bullocks eat the grass on 10 acres in 16 weeks. Therefore, if 6 bullocks keep down the growth on 10 acres, 24 will keep down the growth on 40 acres.

Again, we find that if 6 bullocks eat the accumulated grass on 10 acres in 16 weeks, then

12 eat the grass on	10 acres in	8 weeks,		
48 „	„	40 „	8 „	
192 „	„	40 „	2 „	
64 „	„	40 „	6 „	

Add the two results together (24 + 64), and we find that 88 oxen may be fed on a 40-acre meadow for 6 weeks, the grass growing regularly all the time.

112.—*The Great Grangemoor Mystery.*

We were told that the bullet that killed Mr. Stanton Mowbray struck the very centre of the clock face and instantly welded together the hour, minute, and second hands, so that all revolved in one piece. The puzzle was to tell from the fixed relative positions of the three hands the exact time when the pistol was fired.

We were also told, and the illustration of the clock face bore out the statement, that the hour and minute hands were exactly twenty divisions apart, " the third of the circumference of the dial." Now, there are eleven times in twelve hours when the hour hand is exactly twenty divisions ahead of the minute hand, and eleven times when the minute hand is exactly twenty divisions ahead of the hour hand. The illustration showed that we had only to consider the former case. If we start at four o'clock, and keep on adding 1 h. 5 m. $27\frac{3}{11}$ sec., we shall get all these eleven times, the last being 2 h. 54 min. $32\frac{8}{11}$ sec. Another addition brings us back to four o'clock. If we now examine the clock face, we shall find that the seconds hand is nearly twenty-two divisions behind the minute hand, and if we look at all our eleven times we shall find that only in the last case given above is the seconds hand at this distance. Therefore the shot must have been fired at 2 h. 54 min. $32\frac{8}{11}$ sec. exactly, or, put the other way, at 5 min. $27\frac{3}{11}$ sec. to three o'clock. This is the correct and only possible answer to the puzzle.

113.—*Cutting a Wood Block.*

Though the cubic contents are sufficient for twenty-five pieces, only twenty-four can actually be cut from the block. First reduce the length of the block by half an inch. The smaller piece cut off constitutes the portion that cannot be used. Cut the larger piece into three slabs, each one and a quarter inch thick, and it will be found that eight blocks may easily be cut out of each slab without any further waste.

114.—*The Tramps and the Biscuits.*

The smallest number of biscuits must have been 1021, from which it is evident that they were of that miniature description that finds favour in the nursery. The general solution is that for n men the number must be $m(n^{n+1}) - (n - 1)$, where m is any integer. Each man will receive $m(n - 1)^n - 1$ biscuits at the final division, though in the case of two men, when $m = 1$, the final distribution only benefits the dog. Of course, in every case each man steals an nth of the number of biscuits, after giving the odd one to the dog.

INDEX

251

INDEX

THE END.

A CATALOGUE OF
SELECTED DOVER BOOKS
IN ALL FIELDS OF INTEREST

A CATALOGUE OF SELECTED DOVER BOOKS IN ALL FIELDS OF INTEREST

CELESTIAL OBJECTS FOR COMMON TELESCOPES, T. W. Webb. The most used book in amateur astronomy: inestimable aid for locating and identifying nearly 4,000 celestial objects. Edited, updated by Margaret W. Mayall. 77 illustrations. Total of 645pp. 5⅜ x 8½.
20917-2, 20918-0 Pa., Two-vol. set $9.00

HISTORICAL STUDIES IN THE LANGUAGE OF CHEMISTRY, M. P. Crosland. The important part language has played in the development of chemistry from the symbolism of alchemy to the adoption of systematic nomenclature in 1892. ". . . wholeheartedly recommended,"—Science. 15 illustrations. 416pp. of text. 5⅝ x 8¼. 63702-6 Pa. $6.00

BURNHAM'S CELESTIAL HANDBOOK, Robert Burnham, Jr. Thorough, readable guide to the stars beyond our solar system. Exhaustive treatment, fully illustrated. Breakdown is alphabetical by constellation: Andromeda to Cetus in Vol. 1; Chamaeleon to Orion in Vol. 2; and Pavo to Vulpecula in Vol. 3. Hundreds of illustrations. Total of about 2000pp. 6⅛ x 9¼.
23567-X, 23568-8, 23673-0 Pa., Three-vol. set $26.85

THEORY OF WING SECTIONS: INCLUDING A SUMMARY OF AIR-FOIL DATA, Ira H. Abbott and A. E. von Doenhoff. Concise compilation of subatomic aerodynamic characteristics of modern NASA wing sections, plus description of theory. 350pp. of tables. 693pp. 5⅜ x 8½.
60586-8 Pa. $7.00

DE RE METALLICA, Georgius Agricola. Translated by Herbert C. Hoover and Lou H. Hoover. The famous Hoover translation of greatest treatise on technological chemistry, engineering, geology, mining of early modern times (1556). All 289 original woodcuts. 638pp. 6¾ x 11.
60006-8 Clothbd. $17.50

THE ORIGIN OF CONTINENTS AND OCEANS, Alfred Wegener. One of the most influential, most controversial books in science, the classic statement for continental drift. Full 1966 translation of Wegener's final (1929) version. 64 illustrations. 246pp. 5⅜ x 8½. 61708-4 Pa. $3.00

THE PRINCIPLES OF PSYCHOLOGY, William James. Famous long course complete, unabridged. Stream of thought, time perception, memory, experimental methods; great work decades ahead of its time. Still valid, useful; read in many classes. 94 figures. Total of 1391pp. 5⅜ x 8½.
20381-6, 20382-4 Pa., Two-vol. set $13.00

YUCATAN BEFORE AND AFTER THE CONQUEST, Diego de Landa. First English translation of basic book in Maya studies, the only significant account of Yucatan written in the early post-Conquest era. Translated by distinguished Maya scholar William Gates. Appendices, introduction, 4 maps and over 120 illustrations added by translator. 162pp. 5⅜ x 8½.
23622-6 Pa. $3.00

THE MALAY ARCHIPELAGO, Alfred R. Wallace. Spirited travel account by one of founders of modern biology. Touches on zoology, botany, ethnography, geography, and geology. 62 illustrations, maps. 515pp. 5⅜ x 8½.
20187-2 Pa. $6.95

THE DISCOVERY OF THE TOMB OF TUTANKHAMEN, Howard Carter, A. C. Mace. Accompany Carter in the thrill of discovery, as ruined passage suddenly reveals unique, untouched, fabulously rich tomb. Fascinating account, with 106 illustrations. New introduction by J. M. White. Total of 382pp. 5⅜ x 8½. (Available in U.S. only)   23500-9 Pa. $4.00

THE WORLD'S GREATEST SPEECHES, edited by Lewis Copeland and Lawrence W. Lamm. Vast collection of 278 speeches from Greeks up to present. Powerful and effective models; unique look at history. Revised to 1970. Indices. 842pp. 5⅜ x 8½.   20468-5 Pa. $8.95

THE 100 GREATEST ADVERTISEMENTS, Julian Watkins. The priceless ingredient; His master's voice; 99 44/100% pure; over 100 others. How they were written, their impact, etc. Remarkable record. 130 illustrations. 233pp. 7⅞ x 10 3/5.   20540-1 Pa. $5.00

CRUICKSHANK PRINTS FOR HAND COLORING, George Cruickshank. 18 illustrations, one side of a page, on fine-quality paper suitable for watercolors. Caricatures of people in society (c. 1820) full of trenchant wit. Very large format. 32pp. 11 x 16.   23684-6 Pa. $5.00

THIRTY-TWO COLOR POSTCARDS OF TWENTIETH-CENTURY AMERICAN ART, Whitney Museum of American Art. Reproduced in full color in postcard form are 31 art works and one shot of the museum. Calder, Hopper, Rauschenberg, others. Detachable. 16pp. 8¼ x 11.
23629-3 Pa. $2.50

MUSIC OF THE SPHERES: THE MATERIAL UNIVERSE FROM ATOM TO QUASAR SIMPLY EXPLAINED, Guy Murchie. Planets, stars, geology, atoms, radiation, relativity, quantum theory, light, antimatter, similar topics. 319 figures. 664pp. 5⅜ x 8½.
21809-0, 21810-4 Pa., Two-vol. set $10.00

EINSTEIN'S THEORY OF RELATIVITY, Max Born. Finest semi-technical account; covers Einstein, Lorentz, Minkowski, and others, with much detail, much explanation of ideas and math not readily available elsewhere on this level. For student, non-specialist. 376pp. 5⅜ x 8½.
60769-0 Pa. $4.00

THE COMPLETE BOOK OF DOLL MAKING AND COLLECTING, Catherine Christopher. Instructions, patterns for dozens of dolls, from rag doll on up to elaborate, historically accurate figures. Mould faces, sew clothing, make doll houses, etc. Also collecting information. Many illustrations. 288pp. 6 x 9. 22066-4 Pa. $4.00

THE DAGUERREOTYPE IN AMERICA, Beaumont Newhall. Wonderful portraits, 1850's townscapes, landscapes; full text plus 104 photographs. The basic book. Enlarged 1976 edition. 272pp. 8¼ x 11¼. 23322-7 Pa. $6.00

CRAFTSMAN HOMES, Gustav Stickley. 296 architectural drawings, floor plans, and photographs illustrate 40 different kinds of "Mission-style" homes from The Craftsman (1901-16), voice of American style of simplicity and organic harmony. Thorough coverage of Craftsman idea in text and picture, now collector's item. 224pp. 8⅛ x 11. 23791-5 Pa. $6.00

PEWTER-WORKING: INSTRUCTIONS AND PROJECTS, Burl N. Osborn. & Gordon O. Wilber. Introduction to pewter-working for amateur craftsman. History and characteristics of pewter; tools, materials, step-by-step instructions. Photos, line drawings, diagrams. Total of 160pp. 7⅞ x 10¾. 23736-9 Pa. $3.50

THE GREAT CHICAGO FIRE, edited by David Lowe. 10 dramatic, eye-witness accounts of the 1871 disaster, including one of the aftermath and rebuilding, plus 70 contemporary photographs and illustrations of the ruins—courthouse, Palmer House, Great Central Depot, etc. Introduction by David Lowe. 87pp. 8¼ x 11. 23771-0 Pa. $4.00

SILHOUETTES: A PICTORIAL ARCHIVE OF VARIED ILLUSTRATIONS, edited by Carol Belanger Grafton. Over 600 silhouettes from the 18th to 20th centuries include profiles and full figures of men and women, children, birds and animals, groups and scenes, nature, ships, an alphabet. Dozens of uses for commercial artists and craftspeople. 144pp. 8⅜ x 11¼. 23781-8 Pa. $4.00

ANIMALS: 1,419 COPYRIGHT-FREE ILLUSTRATIONS OF MAMMALS, BIRDS, FISH, INSECTS, ETC., edited by Jim Harter. Clear wood engravings present, in extremely lifelike poses, over 1,000 species of animals. One of the most extensive copyright-free pictorial sourcebooks of its kind. Captions. Index. 284pp. 9 x 12. 23766-4 Pa. $7.50

INDIAN DESIGNS FROM ANCIENT ECUADOR, Frederick W. Shaffer. 282 original designs by pre-Columbian Indians of Ecuador (500-1500 A.D.). Designs include people, mammals, birds, reptiles, fish, plants, heads, geometric designs. Use as is or alter for advertising, textiles, leathercraft, etc. Introduction. 95pp. 8¾ x 11¼. 23764-8 Pa. $3.50

SZIGETI ON THE VIOLIN, Joseph Szigeti. Genial, loosely structured tour by premier violinist, featuring a pleasant mixture of reminiscenes, insights into great music and musicians, innumerable tips for practicing violinists. 385 musical passages. 256pp. 5⅝ x 8¼. 23763-X Pa. $3.50

TONE POEMS, SERIES II: TILL EULENSPIEGELS LUSTIGE STREICHE, ALSO SPRACH ZARATHUSTRA, AND EIN HELDEN-LEBEN, Richard Strauss. Three important orchestral works, including very popular *Till Eulenspiegel's Marry Pranks,* reproduced in full score from original editions. Study score. 315pp. 9⅜ x 12¼. (Available in U.S. only)
23755-9 Pa. $7.50

TONE POEMS, SERIES I: DON JUAN, TOD UND VERKLARUNG AND DON QUIXOTE, Richard Strauss. Three of the most often performed and recorded works in entire orchestral repertoire, reproduced in full score from original editions. Study score. 286pp. 9⅜ x 12¼. (Available in U.S. only)
23754-0 Pa. $7.50

11 LATE STRING QUARTETS, Franz Joseph Haydn. The form which Haydn defined and "brought to perfection." *(Grove's).* 11 string quartets in complete score, his last and his best. The first in a projected series of the complete Haydn string quartets. Reliable modern Eulenberg edition, otherwise difficult to obtain. 320pp. 8⅜ x 11¼. (Available in U.S. only)
23753-2 Pa. $6.95

FOURTH, FIFTH AND SIXTH SYMPHONIES IN FULL SCORE, Peter Ilyitch Tchaikovsky. Complete orchestral scores of Symphony No. 4 in F Minor, Op. 36; Symphony No. 5 in E Minor, Op. 64; Symphony No. 6 in B Minor, "Pathetique," Op. 74. Bretikopf & Hartel eds. Study score. 480pp. 9⅜ x 12¼.
23861-X Pa. $10.95

THE MARRIAGE OF FIGARO: COMPLETE SCORE, Wolfgang A. Mozart. Finest comic opera ever written. Full score, not to be confused with piano renderings. Peters edition. Study score. 448pp. 9⅜ x 12¼. (Available in U.S. only)
23751-6 Pa. $11.95

"IMAGE" ON THE ART AND EVOLUTION OF THE FILM, edited by Marshall Deutelbaum. Pioneering book brings together for first time 38 groundbreaking articles on early silent films from *Image* and 263 illustrations newly shot from rare prints in the collection of the International Museum of Photography. A landmark work. Index. 256pp. 8¼ x 11.
23777-X Pa. $8.95

AROUND-THE-WORLD COOKY BOOK, Lois Lintner Sumption and Marguerite Lintner Ashbrook. 373 cooky and frosting recipes from 28 countries (America, Austria, China, Russia, Italy, etc.) include Viennese kisses, rice wafers, London strips, lady fingers, hony, sugar spice, maple cookies, etc. Clear instructions. All tested. 38 drawings. 182pp. 5⅜ x 8.
23802-4 Pa. $2.50

THE ART NOUVEAU STYLE, edited by Roberta Waddell. 579 rare photographs, not available elsewhere, of works in jewelry, metalwork, glass, ceramics, textiles, architecture and furniture by 175 artists—Mucha, Seguy, Lalique, Tiffany, Gaudin, Hohlwein, Saarinen, and many others. 288pp. 8⅜ x 11¼.
23515-7 Pa. $6.95

THE AMERICAN SENATOR, Anthony Trollope. Little known, long un-available Trollope novel on a grand scale. Here are humorous comment on American vs. English culture, and stunning portrayal of a heroine/villainess. Superb evocation of Victorian village life. 561pp. 5⅜ x 8½.
23801-6 Pa. $6.00

WAS IT MURDER? James Hilton. The author of *Lost Horizon* and *Good-bye, Mr. Chips* wrote one detective novel (under a pen-name) which was quickly forgotten and virtually lost, even at the height of Hilton's fame. This edition brings it back—a finely crafted public school puzzle resplen-dent with Hilton's stylish atmosphere. A thoroughly English thriller by the creator of Shangri-la. 252pp. 5⅜ x 8. (Available in U.S. only)
23774-5 Pa. $3.00

CENTRAL PARK: A PHOTOGRAPHIC GUIDE, Victor Laredo and Henry Hope Reed. 121 superb photographs show dramatic views of Central Park: Bethesda Fountain, Cleopatra's Needle, Sheep Meadow, the Blockhouse, plus people engaged in many park activities: ice skating, bike riding, etc. Captions by former Curator of Central Park, Henry Hope Reed, provide historical view, changes, etc. Also photos of N.Y. landmarks on park's periphery. 96pp. 8½ x 11.
23750-8 Pa. $4.50

NANTUCKET IN THE NINETEENTH CENTURY, Clay Lancaster. 180 rare photographs, stereographs, maps, drawings and floor plans recreate unique American island society. Authentic scenes of shipwreck, light-houses, streets, homes are arranged in geographic sequence to provide walking-tour guide to old Nantucket existing today. Introduction, captions. 160pp. 8⅞ x 11¾.
23747-8 Pa. $6.95

STONE AND MAN: A PHOTOGRAPHIC EXPLORATION, Andreas Feininger. 106 photographs by *Life* photographer Feininger portray man's deep passion for stone through the ages. Stonehenge-like megaliths, forti-fied towns, sculpted marble and crumbling tenements show textures, beau-ties, fascination. 128pp. 9¼ x 10¾.
23756-7 Pa. $5.95

CIRCLES, A MATHEMATICAL VIEW, D. Pedoe. Fundamental aspects of college geometry, non-Euclidean geometry, and other branches of mathe-matics: representing circle by point. Poincare model, isoperimetric prop-erty, etc. Stimulating recreational reading. 66 figures. 96pp. 5⅝ x 8¼.
63698-4 Pa. $2.75

THE DISCOVERY OF NEPTUNE, Morton Grosser. Dramatic scientific history of the investigations leading up to the actual discovery of the eighth planet of our solar system. Lucid, well-researched book by well-known historian of science. 172pp. 5⅜ x 8½. 23726-5 Pa. $3.00

THE DEVIL'S DICTIONARY. Ambrose Bierce. Barbed, bitter, brilliant witticisms in the form of a dictionary. Best, most ferocious satire America has produced. 145pp. 5⅜ x 8½. 20487-1 Pa. $1.75

HISTORY OF BACTERIOLOGY, William Bulloch. The only comprehensive history of bacteriology from the beginnings through the 19th century. Special emphasis is given to biography-Leeuwenhoek, etc. Brief accounts of 350 bacteriologists form a separate section. No clearer, fuller study, suitable to scientists and general readers, has yet been written. 52 illustrations. 448pp. 5⅝ x 8¼. 23761-3 Pa. $6.50

THE COMPLETE NONSENSE OF EDWARD LEAR, Edward Lear. All nonsense limericks, zany alphabets, Owl and Pussycat, songs, nonsense botany, etc., illustrated by Lear. Total of 321pp. 5⅜ x 8½. (Available in U.S. only) 20167-8 Pa. $3.00

INGENIOUS MATHEMATICAL PROBLEMS AND METHODS, Louis A. Graham. Sophisticated material from Graham *Dial*, applied and pure; stresses solution methods. Logic, number theory, networks, inversions, etc. 237pp. 5⅜ x 8½. 20545-2 Pa. $3.50

BEST MATHEMATICAL PUZZLES OF SAM LOYD, edited by Martin Gardner. Bizarre, original, whimsical puzzles by America's greatest puzzler. From fabulously rare *Cyclopedia*, including famous 14-15 puzzles, the Horse of a Different Color, 115 more. Elementary math. 150 illustrations. 167pp. 5⅜ x 8½. 20498-7 Pa. $2.50

THE BASIS OF COMBINATION IN CHESS, J. du Mont. Easy-to-follow, instructive book on elements of combination play, with chapters on each piece and every powerful combination team—two knights, bishop and knight, rook and bishop, etc. 250 diagrams. 218pp. 5⅜ x 8½. (Available in U.S. only) 23644-7 Pa. $3.50

MODERN CHESS STRATEGY, Ludek Pachman. The use of the queen, the active king, exchanges, pawn play, the center, weak squares, etc. Section on rook alone worth price of the book. Stress on the moderns. Often considered the most important book on strategy. 314pp. 5⅜ x 8½. 20290-9 Pa. $3.50

LASKER'S MANUAL OF CHESS, Dr. Emanuel Lasker. Great world champion offers very thorough coverage of all aspects of chess. Combinations, position play, openings, end game, aesthetics of chess, philosophy of struggle, much more. Filled with analyzed games. 390pp. 5⅜ x 8½. 20640-8 Pa. $4.00

500 MASTER GAMES OF CHESS, S. Tartakower, J. du Mont. Vast collection of great chess games from 1798-1938, with much material nowhere else readily available. Fully annotated, arranged by opening for easier study. 664pp. 5⅜ x 8½. 23208-5 Pa. $6.00

A GUIDE TO CHESS ENDINGS, Dr. Max Euwe, David Hooper. One of the finest modern works on chess endings. Thorough analysis of the most frequently encountered endings by former world champion. 331 examples, each with diagram. 248pp. 5⅜ x 8½. 23332-4 Pa. $3.50

SECOND PIATIGORSKY CUP, edited by Isaac Kashdan. One of the greatest tournament books ever produced in the English language. All 90 games of the 1966 tournament, annotated by players, most annotated by both players. Features Petrosian, Spassky, Fischer, Larsen, six others. 228pp. 5⅜ x 8½.   23572-6 Pa. $3.50

ENCYCLOPEDIA OF CARD TRICKS, revised and edited by Jean Hugard. How to perform over 600 card tricks, devised by the world's greatest magicians: impromptus, spelling tricks, key cards, using special packs, much, much more. Additional chapter on card technique. 66 illustrations. 402pp. 5⅜ x 8½. (Available in U.S. only)   21252-1 Pa. $3.95

MAGIC: STAGE ILLUSIONS, SPECIAL EFFECTS AND TRICK PHOTOGRAPHY, Albert A. Hopkins, Henry R. Evans. One of the great classics; fullest, most authorative explanation of vanishing lady, levitations, scores of other great stage effects. Also small magic, automata, stunts. 446 illustrations. 556pp. 5⅜ x 8½.   23344-8 Pa. $5.00

THE SECRETS OF HOUDINI, J. C. Cannell. Classic study of Houdini's incredible magic, exposing closely-kept professional secrets and revealing, in general terms, the whole art of stage magic. 67 illustrations. 279pp. 5⅜ x 8½.   22913-0 Pa. $3.00

HOFFMANN'S MODERN MAGIC, Professor Hoffmann. One of the best, and best-known, magicians' manuals of the past century. Hundreds of tricks from card tricks and simple sleight of hand to elaborate illusions involving construction of complicated machinery. 332 illustrations. 563pp. 5⅜ x 8½.   23623-4 Pa. $6.00

MADAME PRUNIER'S FISH COOKERY BOOK, Mme. S. B. Prunier. More than 1000 recipes from world famous Prunier's of Paris and London, specially adapted here for American kitchen. Grilled tournedos with anchovy butter, Lobster a la Bordelaise, Prunier's prized desserts, more. Glossary. 340pp. 5⅜ x 8½. (Available in U.S. only)   22679-4 Pa. $3.00

FRENCH COUNTRY COOKING FOR AMERICANS, Louis Diat. 500 easy-to-make, authentic provincial recipes compiled by former head chef at New York's Fitz-Carlton Hotel: onion soup, lamb stew, potato pie, more. 309pp. 5⅜ x 8½.   23665-X Pa. $3.95

SAUCES, FRENCH AND FAMOUS, Louis Diat. Complete book gives over 200 specific recipes: bechamel, Bordelaise, hollandaise, Cumberland, apricot, etc. Author was one of this century's finest chefs, originator of vichyssoise and many other dishes. Index. 156pp. 5⅜ x 8.
23663-3 Pa. $2.50

TOLL HOUSE TRIED AND TRUE RECIPES, Ruth Graves Wakefield. Authentic recipes from the famous Mass. restaurant: popovers, veal and ham loaf, Toll House baked beans, chocolate cake crumb pudding, much more. Many helpful hints. Nearly 700 recipes. Index. 376pp. 5⅜ x 8½.
23560-2 Pa. $4.00

CATALOGUE OF DOVER BOOKS

"OSCAR" OF THE WALDORF'S COOKBOOK, Oscar Tschirky. Famous American chef reveals 3455 recipes that made Waldorf great; cream of French, German, American cooking, in all categories. Full instructions, easy home use. 1896 edition. 907pp. 6⅝ x 9⅜.   20790-0 Clothbd. $15.00

COOKING WITH BEER, Carole Fahy. Beer has as superb an effect on food as wine, and at fraction of cost. Over 250 recipes for appetizers, soups, main dishes, desserts, breads, etc. Index. 144pp. 5⅜ x 8½. (Available in U.S. only)   23661-7 Pa. $2.50

STEWS AND RAGOUTS, Kay Shaw Nelson. This international cookbook offers wide range of 108 recipes perfect for everyday, special occasions, meals-in-themselves, main dishes. Economical, nutritious, easy-to-prepare: goulash, Irish stew, boeuf bourguignon, etc. Index. 134pp. 5⅜ x 8½.   23662-5 Pa. $2.50

DELICIOUS MAIN COURSE DISHES, Marian Tracy. Main courses are the most important part of any meal. These 200 nutritious, economical recipes from around the world make every meal a delight. "I . . . have found it so useful in my own household,"—*N.Y. Times.* Index. 219pp. 5⅜ x 8½.   23664-1 Pa. $3.00

FIVE ACRES AND INDEPENDENCE, Maurice G. Kains. Great back-to-the-land classic explains basics of self-sufficient farming: economics, plants, crops, animals, orchards, soils, land selection, host of other necessary things. Do not confuse with skimpy faddist literature; Kains was one of America's greatest agriculturalists. 95 illustrations. 397pp. 5⅜ x 8½.   20974-1 Pa.$3.95

A PRACTICAL GUIDE FOR THE BEGINNING FARMER, Herbert Jacobs. Basic, extremely useful first book for anyone thinking about moving to the country and starting a farm. Simpler than Kains, with greater emphasis on country living in general. 246pp. 5⅜ x 8½.   23675-7 Pa. $3.50

A GARDEN OF PLEASANT FLOWERS (PARADISI IN SOLE: PARADISUS TERRESTRIS), John Parkinson. Complete, unabridged reprint of first (1629) edition of earliest great English book on gardens and gardening. More than 1000 plants & flowers of Elizabethan, Jacobean garden fully described, most with woodcut illustrations. Botanically very reliable, a "speaking garden" of exceeding charm. 812 illustrations. 628pp. 8½ x 12¼.   23392-8 Clothbd. $25.00

ACKERMANN'S COSTUME PLATES, Rudolph Ackermann. Selection of 96 plates from the *Repository of Arts,* best published source of costume for English fashion during the early 19th century. 12 plates also in color. Captions, glossary and introduction by editor Stella Blum. Total of 120pp. 8⅜ x 11¼.   23690-0 Pa. $4.50

MUSHROOMS, EDIBLE AND OTHERWISE, Miron E. Hard. Profusely illustrated, very useful guide to over 500 species of mushrooms growing in the Midwest and East. Nomenclature updated to 1976. 505 illustrations. 628pp. 6½ x 9¼. 23309-X Pa. $7.95

AN ILLUSTRATED FLORA OF THE NORTHERN UNITED STATES AND CANADA, Nathaniel L. Britton, Addison Brown. Encyclopedic work covers 4666 species, ferns on up. Everything. Full botanical information, illustration for each. This earlier edition is preferred by many to more recent revisions. 1913 edition. Over 4000 illustrations, total of 2087pp. 6⅛ x 9¼. 22642-5, 22643-3, 22644-1 Pa., Three-vol. set $24.00

MANUAL OF THE GRASSES OF THE UNITED STATES, A. S. Hitchcock, U.S. Dept. of Agriculture. The basic study of American grasses, both indigenous and escapes, cultivated and wild. Over 1400 species. Full descriptions, information. Over 1100 maps, illustrations. Total of 1051pp. 5⅜ x 8½. 22717-0, 22718-9 Pa., Two-vol. set $12.00

THE CACTACEAE,, Nathaniel L. Britton, John N. Rose. Exhaustive, definitive. Every cactus in the world. Full botanical descriptions. Thorough statement of nomenclatures, habitat, detailed finding keys. The one book needed by every cactus enthusiast. Over 1275 illustrations. Total of 1080pp. 8 x 10¼. 21191-6, 21192-4 Clothbd., Two-vol. set $35.00

AMERICAN MEDICINAL PLANTS, Charles F. Millspaugh. Full descriptions, 180 plants covered: history; physical description; methods of preparation with all chemical constituents extracted; all claimed curative or adverse effects. 180 full-page plates. Classification table. 804pp. 6½ x 9¼. 23034-1 Pa. $10.00

A MODERN HERBAL, Margaret Grieve. Much the fullest, most exact, most useful compilation of herbal material. Gigantic alphabetical encyclopedia, from aconite to zedoary, gives botanical information, medical properties, folklore, economic uses, and much else. Indispensable to serious reader. 161 illustrations. 888pp. 6½ x 9¼. (Available in U.S. only) 22798-7, 22799-5 Pa., Two-vol. set $11.00

THE HERBAL or GENERAL HISTORY OF PLANTS, John Gerard. The 1633 edition revised and enlarged by Thomas Johnson. Containing almost 2850 plant descriptions and 2705 superb illustrations, Gerard's *Herbal* is a monumental work, the book all modern English herbals are derived from, the one herbal every serious enthusiast should have in its entirety. Original editions are worth perhaps $750. 1678pp. 8½ x 12¼. 23147-X Clothbd. $50.00

MANUAL OF THE TREES OF NORTH AMERICA, Charles S. Sargent. The basic survey of every native tree and tree-like shrub, 717 species in all. Extremely full descriptions, information on habitat, growth, locales, economics, etc. Necessary to every serious tree lover. Over 100 finding keys. 783 illustrations. Total of 986pp. 5⅜ x 8½. 20277-1, 20278-X Pa., Two-vol. set $10.00

AMERICAN BIRD ENGRAVINGS, Alexander Wilson et al. All 76 plates. from Wilson's *American Ornithology* (1808-14), most important ornithological work before Audubon, plus 27 plates from the supplement (1825-33) by Charles Bonaparte. Over 250 birds portrayed. 8 plates also reproduced in full color. 111pp. 9⅜ x 12½. 23195-X Pa. $6.00

CRUICKSHANK'S PHOTOGRAPHS OF BIRDS OF AMERICA, Allan D. Cruickshank. Great ornithologist, photographer presents 177 closeups, groupings, panoramas, flightings, etc., of about 150 different birds. Expanded *Wings in the Wilderness*. Introduction by Helen G. Cruickshank. 191pp. 8¼ x 11. 23497-5 Pa. $6.00

AMERICAN WILDLIFE AND PLANTS, A. C. Martin, et al. Describes food habits of more than 1000 species of mammals, birds, fish. Special treatment of important food plants. Over 300 illustrations. 500pp. 5⅜ x 8½. 20793-5 Pa. $4.95

THE PEOPLE CALLED SHAKERS, Edward D. Andrews. Lifetime of research, definitive study of Shakers: origins, beliefs, practices, dances, social organization, furniture and crafts, impact on 19th-century USA, present heritage. Indispensable to student of American history, collector. 33 illustrations. 351pp. 5⅜ x 8½. 21081-2 Pa. $4.00

OLD NEW YORK IN EARLY PHOTOGRAPHS, Mary Black. New York City as it was in 1853-1901, through 196 wonderful photographs from N.-Y. Historical Society. Great Blizzard, Lincoln's funeral procession, great buildings. 228pp. 9 x 12. 22907-6 Pa. $7.95

MR. LINCOLN'S CAMERA MAN: MATHEW BRADY, Roy Meredith. Over 300 Brady photos reproduced directly from original negatives, photos. Jackson, Webster, Grant, Lee, Carnegie, Barnum; Lincoln; Battle Smoke, Death of Rebel Sniper, Atlanta Just After Capture. Lively commentary. 368pp. 8⅜ x 11¼. 23021-X Pa. $8.95

TRAVELS OF WILLIAM BARTRAM, William Bartram. From 1773-8, Bartram explored Northern Florida, Georgia, Carolinas, and reported on wild life, plants, Indians, early settlers. Basic account for period, entertaining reading. Edited by Mark Van Doren. 13 illustrations. 141pp. 5⅜ x 8½. 20013-2 Pa. $4.50

THE GENTLEMAN AND CABINET MAKER'S DIRECTOR, Thomas Chippendale. Full reprint, 1762 style book, most influential of all time; chairs, tables, sofas, mirrors, cabinets, etc. 200 plates, plus 24 photographs of surviving pieces. 249pp. 9⅞ x 12¾. 21601-2 Pa. $6.50

AMERICAN CARRIAGES, SLEIGHS, SULKIES AND CARTS, edited by Don H. Berkebile. 168 Victorian illustrations from catalogues, trade journals, fully captioned. Useful for artists. Author is Assoc. Curator, Div. of Transportation of Smithsonian Institution. 168pp. 8½ x 9½. 23328-6 Pa. $5.00

THE SENSE OF BEAUTY, George Santayana. Masterfully written discussion of nature of beauty, materials of beauty, form, expression; art, literature, social sciences all involved. 168pp. 5⅜ x 8½.   20238-0 Pa. $2.50

ON THE IMPROVEMENT OF THE UNDERSTANDING, Benedict Spinoza. Also contains *Ethics, Correspondence*, all in excellent R. Elwes translation. Basic works on entry to philosophy, pantheism, exchange of ideas with great contemporaries. 402pp. 5⅜ x 8½.   20250-X Pa. $4.50

THE TRAGIC SENSE OF LIFE, Miguel de Unamuno. Acknowledged masterpiece of existential literature, one of most important books of 20th century. Introduction by Madariaga. 367pp. 5⅜ x 8½.
20257-7 Pa. $3.50

THE GUIDE FOR THE PERPLEXED, Moses Maimonides. Great classic of medieval Judaism attempts to reconcile revealed religion (Pentateuch, commentaries) with Aristotelian philosophy. Important historically, still relevant in problems. Unabridged Friedlander translation. Total of 473pp. 5⅜ x 8½.   20351-4 Pa. $5.00

THE I CHING (THE BOOK OF CHANGES), translated by James Legge. Complete translation of basic text plus appendices by Confucius, and Chinese commentary of most penetrating divination manual ever prepared. Indispensable to study of early Oriental civilizations, to modern inquiring reader. 448pp. 5⅜ x 8½.   21062-6 Pa. $4.00

THE EGYPTIAN BOOK OF THE DEAD, E. A. Wallis Budge. Complete reproduction of Ani's papyrus, finest ever found. Full hieroglyphic text, interlinear transliteration, word for word translation, smooth translation. Basic work, for Egyptology, for modern study of psychic matters. Total of 533pp. 6½ x 9¼. (Available in U.S. only)   21866-X Pa. $4.95

THE GODS OF THE EGYPTIANS, E. A. Wallis Budge. Never excelled for richness, fullness: all gods, goddesses, demons, mythical figures of Ancient Egypt; their legends, rites, incarnations, variations, powers, etc. Many hieroglyphic texts cited. Over 225 illustrations, plus 6 color plates. Total of 988pp. 6⅛ x 9¼. (Available in U.S. only)
22055-9, 22056-7 Pa., Two-vol. set $12.00

THE ENGLISH AND SCOTTISH POPULAR BALLADS, Francis J. Child. Monumental, still unsuperseded; all known variants of Child ballads, commentary on origins, literary references, Continental parallels, other features. Added: papers by G. L. Kittredge, W. M. Hart. Total of 2761pp. 6½ x 9¼.
21409-5, 21410-9, 21411-7, 21412-5, 21413-3 Pa., Five-vol. set $37.50

CORAL GARDENS AND THEIR MAGIC, Bronsilaw Malinowski. Classic study of the methods of tilling the soil and of agricultural rites in the Trobriand Islands of Melanesia. Author is one of the most important figures in the field of modern social anthropology. 143 illustrations. Indexes. Total of 911pp. of text. 5⅝ x 8¼. (Available in U.S. only)
23597-1 Pa. $12.95

THE PHILOSOPHY OF HISTORY, Georg W. Hegel. Great classic of Western thought develops concept that history is not chance but a rational process, the evolution of freedom. 457pp. 5⅜ x 8½. 20112-0 Pa. $4.50

LANGUAGE, TRUTH AND LOGIC, Alfred J. Ayer. Famous, clear introduction to Vienna, Cambridge schools of Logical Positivism. Role of philosophy, elimination of metaphysics, nature of analysis, etc. 160pp. 5⅜ x 8½. (Available in U.S. only) 20010-8 Pa. $1.75

A PREFACE TO LOGIC, Morris R. Cohen. Great City College teacher in renowned, easily followed exposition of formal logic, probability, values, logic and world order and similar topics; no previous background needed. 209pp. 5⅜ x 8½. 23517-3 Pa. $3.50

REASON AND NATURE, Morris R. Cohen. Brilliant analysis of reason and its multitudinous ramifications by charismatic teacher. Interdisciplinary, synthesizing work widely praised when it first appeared in 1931. Second (1953) edition. Indexes. 496pp. 5⅜ x 8½. 23633-1 Pa. $6.00

AN ESSAY CONCERNING HUMAN UNDERSTANDING, John Locke. The only complete edition of enormously important classic, with authoritative editorial material by A. C. Fraser. Total of 1176pp. 5⅜ x 8½.
20530-4, 20531-2 Pa., Two-vol. set $14.00

HANDBOOK OF MATHEMATICAL FUNCTIONS WITH FORMULAS, GRAPHS, AND MATHEMATICAL TABLES, edited by Milton Abramowitz and Irene A. Stegun. Vast compendium: 29 sets of tables, some to as high as 20 places. 1,046pp. 8 x 10½. 61272-4 Pa. $14.95

MATHEMATICS FOR THE PHYSICAL SCIENCES, Herbert S. Wilf. Highly acclaimed work offers clear presentations of vector spaces and matrices, orthogonal functions, roots of polynomial equations, conformal mapping, calculus of variations, etc. Knowledge of theory of functions of real and complex variables is assumed. Exercises and solutions. Index. 284pp. 5⅝ x 8¼. 63635-6 Pa. $4.50

THE PRINCIPLE OF RELATIVITY, Albert Einstein et al. Eleven most important original papers on special and general theories. Seven by Einstein, two by Lorentz, one each by Minkowski and Weyl. All translated, unabridged. 216pp. 5⅜ x 8½. 60081-5 Pa. $3.00

THERMODYNAMICS, Enrico Fermi. A classic of modern science. Clear, organized treatment of systems, first and second laws, entropy, thermodynamic potentials, gaseous reactions, dilute solutions, entropy constant. No math beyond calculus required. Problems. 160pp. 5⅜ x 8½.
60361-X Pa. $2.75

ELEMENTARY MECHANICS OF FLUIDS, Hunter Rouse. Classic undergraduate text widely considered to be far better than many later books. Ranges from fluid velocity and acceleration to role of compressibility in fluid motion. Numerous examples, questions, problems. 224 illustrations. 376pp. 5⅝ x 8¼. 63699-2 Pa. $5.00

AN AUTOBIOGRAPHY, Margaret Sanger. Exciting personal account of hard-fought battle for woman's right to birth control, against prejudice, church, law. Foremost feminist document. 504pp. 5⅜ x 8½.
20470-7 Pa. $5.50

MY BONDAGE AND MY FREEDOM, Frederick Douglass. Born as a slave, Douglass became outspoken force in antislavery movement. The best of Douglass's autobiographies. Graphic description of slave life. Introduction by P. Foner. 464pp. 5⅜ x 8½. 22457-0 Pa. $5.00

LIVING MY LIFE, Emma Goldman. Candid, no holds barred account by foremost American anarchist: her own life, anarchist movement, famous contemporaries, ideas and their impact. Struggles and confrontations in America, plus deportation to U.S.S.R. Shocking inside account of persecution of anarchists under Lenin. 13 plates. Total of 944pp. 5⅜ x 8½.
22543-7, 22544-5 Pa., Two-vol. set $9.00

LETTERS AND NOTES ON THE MANNERS, CUSTOMS AND CONDITIONS OF THE NORTH AMERICAN INDIANS, George Catlin. Classic account of life among Plains Indians: ceremonies, hunt, warfare, etc. Dover edition reproduces for first time all original paintings. 312 plates. 572pp. of text. 6⅛ x 9¼. 22118-0, 22119-9 Pa.. Two-vol. set $10.00

THE MAYA AND THEIR NEIGHBORS, edited by Clarence L. Hay, others. Synoptic view of Maya civilization in broadest sense, together with Northern, Southern neighbors. Integrates much background, valuable detail not elsewhere. Prepared by greatest scholars: Kroeber, Morley, Thompson, Spinden, Vaillant, many others. Sometimes called Tozzer Memorial Volume. 60 illustrations, linguistic map. 634pp. 5⅜ x 8½.
23510-6 Pa. $7.50

HANDBOOK OF THE INDIANS OF CALIFORNIA, A. L. Kroeber. Foremost American anthropologist offers complete ethnographic study of each group. Monumental classic. 459 illustrations, maps. 995pp. 5⅜ x 8½.
23368-5 Pa. $10.00

SHAKTI AND SHAKTA, Arthur Avalon. First book to give clear, cohesive analysis of Shakta doctrine, Shakta ritual and Kundalini Shakti (yoga). Important work by one of world's foremost students of Shaktic and Tantric thought. 732pp. 5⅜ x 8½. (Available in U.S. only)
23645-5 Pa. $7.95

AN INTRODUCTION TO THE STUDY OF THE MAYA HIEROGLYPHS, Syvanus Griswold Morley. Classic study by one of the truly great figures in hieroglyph research. Still the best introduction for the student for reading Maya hieroglyphs. New introduction by J. Eric S. Thompson. 117 illustrations. 284pp. 5⅜ x 8½. 23108-9 Pa. $4.00

A STUDY OF MAYA ART, Herbert J. Spinden. Landmark classic interprets Maya symbolism, estimates styles, covers ceramics, architecture, murals, stone carvings as artforms. Still a basic book in area. New introduction by J. Eric Thompson. Over 750 illustrations. 341pp. 8⅜ x 11¼.
21235-1 Pa. $6.95

THE STANDARD BOOK OF QUILT MAKING AND COLLECTING, Marguerite Ickis. Full information, full-sized patterns for making 46 traditional quilts, also 150 other patterns. Quilted cloths, lame, satin quilts, etc. 483 illustrations. 273pp. 6⅞ x 9⅝. 20582-7 Pa. $4.50

ENCYCLOPEDIA OF VICTORIAN NEEDLEWORK, S. Caulfield, Blanche Saward. Simply inexhaustible gigantic alphabetical coverage of every traditional needlecraft—stitches, materials, methods, tools, types of work; definitions, many projects to be made. 1200 illustrations; double-columned text. 697pp. 8⅛ x 11. 22800-2, 22801-0 Pa., Two-vol. set $12.00

MECHANICK EXERCISES ON THE WHOLE ART OF PRINTING, Joseph Moxon. First complete book (1683-4) ever written about typography, a compendium of everything known about printing at the latter part of 17th century. Reprint of 2nd (1962) Oxford Univ. Press edition. 74 illustrations. Total of 550pp. 6⅛ x 9¼. 23617-X Pa. $7.95

PAPERMAKING, Dard Hunter. Definitive book on the subject by the foremost authority in the field. Chapters dealing with every aspect of history of craft in every part of the world. Over 320 illustrations. 2nd, revised and enlarged (1947) edition. 672pp. 5⅜ x 8½. 23619-6 Pa. $7.95

THE ART DECO STYLE, edited by Theodore Menten. Furniture, jewelry, metalwork, ceramics, fabrics, lighting fixtures, interior decors, exteriors, graphics from pure French sources. Best sampling around. Over 400 photographs. 183pp. 8⅜ x 11¼. 22824-X Pa. $5.00

Prices subject to change without notice.

Available at your book dealer or write for free catalogue to Dept. GI, Dover Publications, Inc., 180 Varick St., N.Y., N.Y. 10014. Dover publishes more than 175 books each year on science, elementary and advanced mathematics, biology, music, art, literary history, social sciences and other areas.